THE PLAINS OF HIS HEART

THE PLANS OF HIS HEART

Understanding How You Fit Into God's Perfect Will

CHIP RICKS

BROADMAN & HOLMAN PUBLISHERS

Nashville, Tennessee

4262-70
0-8054-6270-8

Published by Broadman & Holman Publishers, Nashville, Tennessee
Acquisitions & Development Editor: Vicki Crumpton
Design by Leslie Joslin

Dewey Decimal Classification: 231.5
Subject Heading: GOD—WILL / CHRISTIAN LIFE
Library of Congress Card Catalog Number: 95-14496

Library of Congress Cataloging-in-Publication Data
Ricks, Chip.
      The plans of His heart : understanding how you fit into God's perfect will / Chip Ricks
         p.   cm.
      Includes bibliographical references.
      ISBN 0-8054-6270-8 (pbk.)
      1. Providence and government of God. 2. God—Will.
      3. Spiritual life—Baptists. 4. Baptists—Doctrines. I. Title
BT135.R53   1996
231.7—dc20

96-14496
CIP

00 99 98 97 96 5 4 3 2 1

*To my loving husband, Al,
whose invaluable support, gentle guidance,
and consistent life of Christian service
have inspired me and made this book possible.*

Acknowledgments

Thanks to:

My son Rick, my "family" editor. There was a time when I taught you to read and write. Now you're teaching me.

My editor, Vicki Crumpton. You never gave up on me as I struggled through some changes. I appreciate you!

My TLC group. Your prayers and encouragement have kept my heart at ease. I love you all.

Contents

Contents

Part 3 / The Response of His Children

Preface

There are times in all our lives when we feel frustrated because we don't understand what God is doing in the world. We read the daily newspaper or listen to Dan Rather or Ted Koppel report the news, and we wonder if God has forgotten us. Our society is changing, and we're not sure who is responsible for the chaos we see all around us. We may even feel like the prophet Habakkuk when he cried out in total abandon:

> How long, O LORD, must I call for help,
>   but you do not listen? Or cry out to you,
> "Violence!" but you do not save?
> Why do you make me look at injustice?
> Why do you tolerate wrong? (1:2–3)

We look at our personal lives and wonder why we didn't get a certain job, why we have to move across the country away from everyone we love, or why tragedy has struck our family. Why are our carefully laid plans not working out? We relate to Dante's words in *The Divine Comedy* when he said, "Midway upon the journey of our life I found myself in a dark wood, where the right way was lost."

But there's good news! We don't have to stay in the dark woods. God has a plan for the world He created. And He has a plan for His people. The exciting news is that we can be a part of that plan—each one of us! If you've taken a detour, gone down the wrong road, you can turn around. If you've never found the right path, you can find it. God's anxious for us to find our place in His plan.

From the beginning God planned a family that would include people from all generations. David wrote in Psalm 33:11, "The counsel of the LORD stands forever, the plans of His heart to all generations" (NKJV). We need to get hold of that plan and understand our part in it. His plan applies to the deepest needs of our daily lives. Following it can lead us out of the dark woods and give us a fresh sense of direction. Only then can we find security and joy and peace as we live out our lives in a world that has lost sight of God's plan.

Part 1
The Depth of His Love

1

The Search for Meaning
in a Changing, Chaotic World

I grew up in a small town in central Texas during the 1930s and 1940s, and I never set foot out of the Lone Star State until I married. As a youngster, my friends were my two sisters, four cousins, and half a dozen neighborhood children. I didn't know what a baby-sitter was because my grandmother lived with us, and aunts and uncles were always available if Mother and Dad had to be away at the same time. Most often my sisters and I just went along.

Social life for our family centered around the First Southern Baptist Church. We never missed a meeting. There was church on Sundays, morning and night. Prayer meeting on Wednesday night. Weeklong revival on the church lawn or on the banks of Little River in the summer. Church suppers. Picnics. Baseball.

Most of the teachers in our schools grew up in Cameron or in one of the nearby communities. They knew our parents. They attended our church. Each school day began with prayer and Bible reading. We memorized as much of God's Word in the public school classroom as we did in Sunday school. I can still recite many of the psalms as well as the Christmas story from Luke 2.

No one ever thought of moving from my hometown. Cameron was a farming and ranching community, and the land was handed down from father to son. Those who went off to college almost always returned to farm, raise cattle, run the local bank, or open a new store.

We felt safe and secure. No one locked their doors, and neighbors were welcome to come in to borrow a cup of sugar, corn meal, or flour whether or not the family was home. We looked out for each other. When I was in high school, many evenings ended with a soda at Denson's Drug Store. I knew Mr. Denson was watching and would report any questionable behavior to my parents. The townspeople kept a close eye on their teenagers.

A World of Rapid Change

Then came World War II. Everything changed. There was a mass exodus of young men eighteen and over. McCloskey Hospital was built almost overnight in the little town of Temple just twenty-six miles away. A plant to make war materials opened in Rockdale, ten miles closer. Every able-bodied man and woman went to work in one or the other if they were not called to the military or needed on the farms, ranches, or the few jobs necessary to keep our town running. Almost every conversation among adults closed with, "We've got to keep life as normal as possible for the children."

But life wasn't normal. And it would never be the same again. I married a lieutenant from the big city of Houston when I was still in my teens and joined him at Williams Army Air Base in Chandler, Arizona. We were there only a year. All fourteen of the places we lived in the next few years were temporary. During our years of air force life, our three children attended eleven different schools in ten different states from California to Maine and from Florida to Montana. Their dad was often away for short tours of duty—three months, six months, a year. Nothing was guaranteed to stay the same—not schools, not houses, not friends, not family, not churches.

Since the close of World War II, life has moved at an even faster pace. Today we can have breakfast in Los Angeles and lunch in New York by traveling in a supersonic jet aircraft. Or we can continue our journey across the ocean and have dinner in London. The invention of fiber optics, transistors, and microcomputers has opened up communication for business around the world. The Polaroid camera, compact disk player, and VHS system have added to our pleasure. The discovery of the polio vaccine and the eradication of smallpox have assured us of healthier lives. And these are but dots on a huge screen of progress we have seen in the past fifty years.

But even though my children grew up with all these things, somehow they had a yearning for the stable life I knew as a child. With all our moving, they considered Cameron and the house where their grandparents lived "home." Later, they all went back to Texas, back "home," to attend college. Why?

Most of us have a deep desire to hold our family units together. Some of us would be content to go back to the time when life moved at a slower pace. In 1995 our family had a reunion at my sister's home, the Beaver Ranch, an hour north of Dallas. All forty members of the Wilson clan were there, but we had to give them weeks of notice since they came from six different states in the Union! There was a time when my aunts, uncles, and cousins by the dozens could be gathered on short notice for an evening together or for lunch when they were in town doing Saturday shopping. Those days are past.

No, we can't go back to the "good old days." We live in the nineties; and along with the many inventions of man that have improved our lives, much has come to trouble us. We can't ignore the distances we must travel to see family and friends. We can't erase the concrete super highways that crisscross our land moving us in all directions, forcing us onto a fast track. Computer viruses haunt us. So do nuclear, chemical, and biological weapons. We can't dispute the prediction of sociologists that the average person working today will change jobs at least seven times during his lifetime. We cannot permanently solve the problem of drugs, violence, theft, or scams. Despite all of our newly acquired knowledge and technology, we have been unable to eliminate terrorism or to prevent civil and international wars. Because the world has been brought to our shores, we can't turn our backs on starving people in Somalia, Zaire, or Bosnia when the storage bins in our own country are filled with grain. The world is wide open, and we can't close the door.

Our Search for Security

Even if we live in a small town in the south, on a ranch far away from the violence of a big city, or on one of the Hawaiian islands, we can't escape the dangers, the problems, the decisions that hover over us. How, then, do we find meaning for our lives in such a changing, chaotic world? Is anything permanent? Lasting? Where is our anchor? Our security?

Many people think security lies in worldly possessions. That's the American dream: a three bedroom house, two cars in the garage, closets full of clothes, china, silverware, and jewelry. When the house is full, enlarge the vision. Buy a bigger house or move to the suburbs. Get an acre, maybe two, and settle in—until the children start growing and growing. Then it's time to move again. The dream now calls for four bedrooms, a recreation room, and ten acres for a horse. Are we ever satisfied? Not really. Secure? Never. Are worldly possessions lasting? No. They can all be destroyed in the blink of an eye by fire, flood, or earthquake.

I remember the night of October 9, 1994. Our family was on vacation in Connecticut when we received a phone call from our neighbor about a fire raging across the fields not far from our home in California. "We've been warned that we'll have to evacuate if the winds don't change," Gene said. "What do you want us to take out of your house?" The words struck fear in our hearts as we thought of the years of accumulated treasures in our home. Pictures of our children from the day they were born, favorite blankets and toys packed away and labeled with dates, books with notes scribbled in the margins. As a military wife, I'd collected momentoes from all over the world—a pair of ivory candlesticks from Italy, a silver spoon from a little shop in Lakenheath, England, a picture painted by an unknown artist in Holland. We'd built much of our home with our own hands. The leaded windows in our family room and front door, the brick around the wood stove in my office, the fresh paint on all the walls—these were labors of love. Was all our labor to be for nothing? I was sure that it was—especially when the words of the Lord in Habakkuk 2:13 came to my mind: "'The people's labor is only fuel for the fire'"! You can imagine how thankful I was when a few hours after that frightening phone call, the winds changed and our home was saved.

Soon after we returned home to California, however, storms struck our state. On January 10, rains came down in torrents, overflowing the rivers and rushing through homes and businesses in Santa Barbara, Ventura, and Los Angeles counties. Thousands of people saw everything they had worked for all their lives destroyed in a few hours. The estimated value of the accumulated worldly goods destroyed was in the millions of dollars.

Then only a few days later, on January 17, the media flashed the news that a devastating earthquake had struck Kobe, Japan. Close to 5,000 people lost their lives, and more than 300,000 were left homeless. The estimated value of property destroyed ran in the billions.

None of this makes sense. Nothing we accumulate on earth is permanent—not as long as we have fires, floods, and earthquakes. Do we really want our lives to be anchored to worldly goods? I vote no.

Could money be an anchor? We can put our money in the bank. We can even watch it grow by investing in stocks and bonds. Don't we have laws to keep our money safe? Let me tell you about Bob whose story made the headlines in our newspaper not long ago.

Bob was only twenty-one when he became a stockbroker. He'd always been interested in making money—lots of it. His father was a sharecropper, a poor man with a big heart. While growing up, Bob thought everyone took advantage of his dad, and he vowed that this would never happen to him. He wanted to be the one on top. That was his goal: to make money, gain respect, and rise to the top. Bob reached every goal he set for himself, but he wasn't satisfied. He wanted more and more money. He took greater and greater risks. The day came when he lost everything, and he could find no reason for living. His world crashed in upon him. At age forty-two he ended his life, unable to face the future in a chaotic world. That was the day he made the headlines in our paper.

Barry Minkow is another one who chose making money and climbing to the top as his purpose for living. He was only sixteen when he started a business in his garage. Five years later it had grown, on paper, into a fortune of $109 million; but Barry had only a short time to enjoy his money, his Ferrari, and his home in Woodland Hills, California. On March 27, 1989, a federal judge sentenced him to twenty-five years in prison and ordered him to repay

$26 million to victims of his ZZZZ Best carpet-cleaning fraud. On the day of his sentencing, the *Los Angeles Times* reported a statement that Barry made to the court: "'To me," he said, "winning meant everything, at all costs. Prestige, power, money, and winning . . . .'"

I don't know about you, but I don't want to anchor my life to money or prestige or power. These can only take us downhill—fast.

Maybe a good job can provide the security we seek. Oh, not just any job. I mean a job that we enjoy—a job that adds one challenge after another, one that keeps us stimulated and moving. Sounds good to me.

Of course, we have to watch our time. If we're not careful, the job can take over, become an obsession, and push everything else out of our lives. It might even take a crisis for us to realize that we're on the fast track, running at full speed, perhaps headed down a dead-end street.

My friend Sam is a prime example. He was caught up in his work for years—the years his kids were growing up and his wife needed him the most. Then one day he got a call from the police. His son had been picked up on a drug charge. When he arrived home after bailing out his son, his wife hit him with years of built-up emotions. She threatened to leave him if things didn't change—soon. So Sam bought a vacation home on the beach and promised to spend the summer months there with his family; however, his promise didn't last. Soon he was commuting from the beach to the office every day. How could he slow down if he wanted to get ahead in the world? In the end his family turned away from him. Sam was alone.

So far our search has led us to consider worldly goods, money, and work as possible goals that might satisfy the longing for meaning in our lives. None of these pass the test as strong anchors or as rocks of security. What else can we try?

Education. Did you ever know a student who couldn't get out of school? It was not because he wasn't intelligent.

Not because he made bad grades. No, it was because he couldn't stop seeking knowledge. I know someone like that. Ken made top grades in every subject he studied. He was always on the honor roll. When he left high school, he went to college with full intention of completing a bachelor of arts in history in four years; but four years stretched into five, then six. His degrees went from B.A. to M.A. to Ph.D. Not yet satisfied, he changed paths and got an M.S. in international relations and then a doctorate in the same field. He was a perpetual student. There was never enough knowledge to satisfy. Never enough.

Suicide is one of the ten leading causes of death in the United States. More than 31,000 people ended their own lives in 1993.[1] Thousands more are walking around today living but not living—spiritually dead. People seeking some meaning for their lives but headed in the wrong direction. People walking down the path to worldly possessions, to money and power and prestige. People striving for jobs that offer more and more challenge or education that provides more and more knowledge. Their stories are found in your daily newspapers. They fill the pages of news magazines. They live in your town and walk your streets. They live next door to you. Some sit next to you in church. You may even be one of them.

Where can we find meaning to our lives when all around us the world is in chaos? Where is our security when we are shuffled from job to job? When we are uprooted from familiar places and faces? When disaster or illness strikes? Who can calm our fears when drive-by shootings occur on the highways we travel? When strangers wait in restrooms to grab our children? When schools teach what contradicts our families' values and the media compromises the truth? Who can we trust?

Only God. He has a plan. When we can't make order out of chaos, God's plan is still at work in our world. It is woven through the history of His people and is worked out in the lives of those who answer His call. He's eager for us to hear that He has a plan for our lives. He never stops calling. His plan is our anchor, our security, our peace. It can never be uprooted. It will never change, and it will bring order and purpose and treasure that can never be destroyed.

We can live our lives in peace and security even in the midst of a chaotic world. More than two thousand years ago a famous king of Israel, King David, saw his world turned upside down. His kingdom was at war. He was guilty of planning a murder and guilty of adultery. David's son Amnon raped his half sister. Another son, Absalom, was killed in battle while leading a rebellion. His family, his kingdom, and his life were all in shambles; but King David knew where to turn for help. "When my spirit was overwhelmed within me," he wrote, "then thou knewest my path" (Ps. 142:3, KJV). David knew that God's plan stretched far beyond Israel and one man's life. Indeed, David wrote, "The counsel of the LORD stands forever, the plans of His heart from generation to generation" (Ps. 33:11, NKJV). Our God has a plan—a plan for the world, a plan for you, a plan for me—and that plan will give meaning to our lives.

Discovering His Plans

1. What cultural changes have you experienced as you moved from childhood to adulthood? What things would you like to preserve from your childhood's culture?

2. In what areas have you searched for meaning for your life: Money? Work? Worldly possessions? Other? Did any of these satisfy?

3. How would you describe the focus and meaning of your life today?

4. Why do you think it is important that you know and understand God's plan for the world and for your life?

2

God's Covenant Plan from Generation to Generation

Few people died in the hospital in the spring of 1941, at least not in central Texas. Almost everyone wanted to breathe their last breath at home, and most did. Grandma never did go to the hospital. When her heart stopped doing what it was supposed to do, she just went to bed.

Old Doctor Denson stopped by every day to see her. He checked her pulse and listened to her heart. Then one morning he said, "Well, Elizabeth, you know as well as I do that your worn-out heart isn't pumping as it used to. One day soon it's just going to stop ticking. You best get prepared to join your Maker." Doctors didn't mince words in those days, but Grandma wouldn't have wanted it any other way.

One night as I sat by her bed quietly listening to her breathe and counting the seconds between breaths, Grandma suddenly opened her eyes and looked right at me. "Honey," she said, "I think my Lord is coming for me tonight, but I don't want you to be afraid. Just imagine a beautiful, white sail boat coming across that glassy sea. Picture your Grandma standing on the shore and Jesus standing in that boat. Do you see Him? His hand is reaching out for me. I'll just put my hand in His and He'll help me aboard. He'll see me safely to the other side."

When tears filled my eyes, Grandma reached up her hand and touched my face. "Now, don't you be sad," she said. "I can't wait to see what my Lord has ready for me. Just remember that He has a plan for this old world, and He has a plan for you. Follow the path He's laid out for your life, and it will work out just right. You'll see. Then someday He'll come for you, and I'll be waiting on the other side of that sea—waiting to give you a big hug!"

It wasn't so much the words that Grandma said as it was the expression on her face that made such an impact on me. I knew she loved me, but I also knew she couldn't wait to get to that other shore.

For Grandma, each day was an adventure—much suffering and hardship, few of life's comforts, but lots of peace and love and assurance. She talked over every problem with the Lord and did what He told her to do. You see, Grandma was just a young girl when God called her into His family. She asked Him to work out His plan in her life. He did. She didn't worry or fret about what each day would bring. She didn't worry about the future either. She just stayed on the right path. She knew where she was going.

It is no secret that God planned an orderly universe and a life of peace for us from the very beginning. Our life is short. King David said life is "like grass; as a flower of the field, so he flourishes. For the wind passes over it, and it is gone" (Ps. 103:15–16, NKJV). We certainly don't want to waste the brief time that we have struggling along down a dead-end path, detouring at every turn hoping to find a better way. God has a perfect plan for us, and He has promised to direct our steps. Remember what the wise King Solomon wrote? "Trust in the LORD with all your heart, and lean not on your own understanding; in all your ways acknowledge Him, and He shall direct your paths" (Prov. 3:5–6, NKJV). God's plan for the world and for His family is not new. He had a plan from the beginning.

God's Plan in the Beginning

In the Book of Genesis, the story of creation opens with a flurry of activity and words. Almost immediately we sense the power, the creativity, and the intelligence of the One who created the universe. "In the beginning God . . . ." He is the central focus, the One who by His word called into existence all that is. I like how Joseph Parker describes it: "The action never pauses for a moment; how busy are the days, and how active the night in star-lighting; in the waters is a great stir of life; the woods are burning with colour; the earth is alive with things that creep; the air vibrates with the clap of wings."[1]

It was a perfect environment. Today when we see the majesty of the redwood forests and then touch the velvet delicacy of a rose, we marvel at the creative mind of God; but most unique of all God's creations was man.

In His Image

> God said, "Let Us make man in Our image, according to Our likeness; let them have dominion over the fish of the sea, over the birds of the air, and over the cattle, over all the earth and over every creeping thing that creeps on the earth." So God created man in His own image; in the image of God He created him; male and female He created them. Then God blessed them, and God said to them, "Be fruitful and multiply." (Gen. 1:26–27, NKJV)

I find it difficult to get past those first few words: "In Our image, according to Our likeness." How overwhelming to think that we are made in the image of God, and the words cause us to search for a truthful meaning. Certainly we are not "little gods" as some religions would have us believe. No, the image of God refers to those qualities He possesses that He has given to us.

First, we were created as spiritual beings capable of a personal relationship with God. Jesus said, "God is spirit," and in our spirits we reach out to God. We can communicate with Him and He with us. We are capable of hearing Him when He calls us and of learning from Him. Second, we were created as moral beings knowing that which is good and right and holy. God intended that we look out for the welfare of other human beings and be concerned about all of His creation. Third, we were created as intellectual beings. Like God, we are creative; we have the ability to rule, to think, to reason, and to make choices. We are His representatives on the earth. Our great creative God has trusted us with this awesome responsibility.

For His Family

"In Our image." I like to think of that image as including the family concept. Our Triune God was present at the creation: one God, yet a community. The Holy Spirit was "hovering over the face of the waters," working in concert with the Father, and the Son was present. John tells us that He was there "in the beginning," and "all things were made through Him" (John 1:2–3, NKJV).

The love of our Triune God shines through the story of creation. Human beings, God's special creation, were spiritual, moral, and intellectual beings. This was not true of other creatures. Created "in His image" tells us that God wants a close relationship with us. He wants our companionship. He wants us to be His family. This was His plan from the beginning.

La Parisima Mission, one of the twenty-one missions in California, was established by the Spanish in 1787. This beautiful mission is near my home. I love to go there early in the morning when the sun is just peeping over the mountains and find my favorite spot on a bench under a tree in the far south garden. Few people go to this area. I sit quietly and wait. Soon the birds begin their symphony of song. The leaves rustle with a gentle breeze, and some sheep grazing on a nearby hill add their soft "amen." Here, I can sense the presence of God in a special way.

Imagine meeting God in the most beautiful place you have ever been. He walks with you, talks with you, and laughs with you. You never want to leave. I imagine that's how it was with Adam and Eve.

God's Plan Rejected

God wanted more, however, for His family. He wanted us to be free, to make choices, to choose to answer His call to come and walk with Him—or to walk alone, out of the garden. I suppose at times we wish our children were not free to choose. Then they would do exactly as we say, never argue, and never make decisions that we know won't work. We don't want mindless robots for children. Neither does God. Being with Him is a gift that we must choose either to accept or reject. We can choose to walk with Him, to love Him, and to obey Him. Or we can choose to go our own way.

What Man Did

Adam and Eve, the first man and the first woman, made the second choice—to disobey God and go their own way. It happened in the garden where the young couple lived. Satan, once an angel who served God, had been thrown out of heaven because he tried to take God's place. Now he appeared to Eve as a crafty, deceitful serpent.

> He said to the woman, "Has God indeed said, 'You shall not eat of every tree in the garden'?"

And the woman said to the serpent, "We may eat the fruit of the trees of the garden; but of the fruit of the tree which is in the midst of the garden, God has said, 'You shall not eat it, nor shall you touch it, lest you die.'"

Then the serpent said to the woman, "You will not surely die. For God knows that in the day you eat of it your eyes will be opened, and you will be like God, knowing good and evil." (Gen. 3:1–5, NKJV)

Satan told Eve that God's word was not true! Does that sound familiar? After all these years some people still argue about the truth of God's Word, and many are still falling into Satan's trap—like Eve. "So when the woman saw that the tree was good for food, that it was pleasant to the eyes, and a tree desirable to make one wise, she took of its fruit and ate. She also gave to her husband with her, and he ate" (Gen. 3:6, NKJV).

Eve chose to believe Satan rather than God. She ate the forbidden fruit and persuaded Adam to do the same. I remember a time when I was angry with Eve for the decision she made, but I now understand that at one time in our lives we've all made that same choice. We've disobeyed God, turned away from Him, and eaten the forbidden fruit. God's plan was that man and woman would live forever, but they brought the penalty of death on themselves by the choice of listening to Satan rather than God.

What God Did

God must have known this would happen. That's why His plan had a provision to redeem us from this sentence of eternal death. He loves us. And He has never given up His plan to have a close relationship with us. He has never stopped calling His people to come to Him. Neither will He take away our freedom to choose whether or not we want to be a part of His family and to have that close relationship with Him. The first insight into understanding

God's plan of redemption comes in His words to the serpent:

"I will put enmity
Between you and the woman,
And between your seed and her Seed;
He shall bruise your head,
And you shall bruise His heel." (Gen. 3:15, NKJV)

Two sides: God's and Satan's. A battle for our souls. God had a plan to win the battle. A Redeemer would conquer death and defeat Satan, but first God had to teach us how costly this redemption was. He began with Adam and Eve.

There's little doubt that they felt guilty and ashamed. They hid and tried to cover themselves with fig leaves, but God covered the sinful couple with tunics of skin. It was the first blood sacrifice, a life for their lives, and a foreshadowing of His plan.

Adam and Eve's two sons, Cain and Abel, are good examples of the choices generations who followed them would make. Both Cain and Abel brought sacrifices to God. Abel was a shepherd and brought the firstborn of his flock, an acceptable sacrificial offering. Cain was a farmer and brought produce he had grown as his offering. Because Cain's offering required no sacrifice, it was not acceptable to God. Cain wasn't willing to follow God's plan. He wanted his own solution to the problem of sin. God tenderly tried to teach Cain the right way. God asked: "'Why are you angry? Why is your face downcast? If you do what is right, will you not be accepted? But if you do not do what is right, sin is crouching at your door; it desires to have you, but you must master it'" (Gen. 4:6–7).

Our God is always willing to teach us. He wanted so much to teach Cain. But Cain was not willing. He was angry, and he was jealous of his brother. His disobedience and rejection, his anger and jealousy, led him to attack Abel in the field and kill him. Cain made his choice.

God's Plan Renewed

Renewed with Noah

Much later, following a great flood in which disobedient people who had followed in the footsteps of Cain were destroyed, a righteous man named Noah built an altar and sacrificed clean animals to the Lord. The Lord was pleased and made a covenant with Noah. "'I will never again curse the ground for man's sake although the imagination of man's heart is evil from his youth; nor will I again destroy every living thing as I have done'" (Gen. 8:21, NKJV). Then God promised a nucleus of order and stability to our world:

"While the earth remains,
Seedtime and harvest,
Cold and heat,
Winter and summer,
And day and night
Shall not cease." (Gen. 8:22, NKJV)

This covenant was not just for Noah and his sons. God said to Noah, "'I establish My covenant with you and with your descendants after you'" (Gen. 9:9, NKJV). Then as a sign of His covenant, God set His rainbow in the sky. We see this sign today and know He has not forgotten.

Renewed with Abraham

It may seem strange to us that as people multiplied on the earth, so many chose to ignore God and to go their own way. Yet it's not very different from today, but always a few have been faithful. Abraham was. God made a covenant with him. Abraham was to obey God. God, in turn, promised Abraham four things: (1) he would have numerous descendants; (2) he would be blessed by God; (3) his name would be great; (4) and he would be a blessing to others. This fourth promise implied the coming of the

Messiah through Abraham's descendants. Later, God promised Abraham a son.

Fourteen years later when God renewed the covenant, Abraham's name was changed from Abram to Abraham, and circumcision was established as a sign of the covenant. This covenant was passed to Isaac, Jacob, and Joseph—generation to generation to generation.

Renewed with His People

Israel was the name God gave to Jacob. God made a covenant with the nation of his descendants, called Israelites. God had not forgotten His covenant, His plan to redeem His people and bring order back into the world He had created. His people were in bondage, and He called Moses to lead them out of Egypt, across the Red Sea, and to Mount Sinai. There God said to them, "'If you will indeed obey My voice, and keep My covenant, then you shall be a special treasure to Me above all people'" (Exod. 19:5, NKJV). God gave these Israelites the Ten Commandments, and the people promised to obey them.

But God did more. He gave them detailed instructions that Moses wrote down in a Book of the Covenant to help them obey and to teach them about His plan to redeem them from eternal death. If they would obey, He promised to care for them, to protect them against their enemies, and to bring them into the promised land. What more could they ask?

God reminded His people, "'I will remember My covenant with Jacob, and My covenant with Isaac and My covenant with Abraham I will remember'" (Lev. 26:42, NKJV). He promised never to cast them away or to break His covenant with them (Lev. 26:44). They had few possessions and no home; they were in the desert surrounded by enemies, but God was there. For those who trusted God's plan, there was peace and security. A remnant answered His call to come to a place of rest in the midst of chaos.

Renewed with David

About a thousand years after God made a covenant with Abraham, He renewed that covenant with David by giving him more details of His plan. The Redeemer, God said, would come through David's seed. In Psalm 89:3–4, God sealed the covenant: "I have made a covenant with My chosen, I have sworn to My servant David: 'Your seed I will establish forever, And build up your throne to all generations'" (NKJV).

Did David understand all that God shared with him? We don't know, but we do know that every detail of God's covenant plan would be fulfilled.

Over and over again in the Old Testament we are told that the people who knew about the covenant God had made with them chose not to obey Him. They refused to keep His covenant. They made graven images, worshiped Baal, and sacrificed their children to idols; but God loved them. He kept watch over them because of His covenant with Abraham, Isaac, and Jacob, and He called to them:

"Ho! Everyone who thirsts,
Come to the waters; . . .
Listen carefully to Me, and eat what is good.
And let your soul delight itself in abundance. . . .
Hear, and your soul shall live." (Isa. 55:1–3, NKJV)

There was always a remnant, a few who came to the waters, who heard and obeyed God. One was King Josiah. God's heart must have rejoiced when this Judean king called his people together and read them the words of the covenant. Hearing those words had a powerful effect on Josiah. He "made a covenant before the LORD, to follow the LORD and to keep His commandments and His testimonies and His statutes, with all his heart and all his soul, to perform the words of this covenant that were written in this book. And all the people took a stand for the covenant" (2 Kings 23:3, NKJV).

The old covenant was not easy to keep—not even for the remnant who chose to follow God's plan and earnestly desired to please Him. No excuse for disobeying the commandments or failing to keep the sacrifices and feasts was acceptable.

God's love for His people was so great, however, that He could not abandon His plan to save them. God's prophets—Isaiah, Jeremiah, Ezekiel—announced His promise of a new covenant. The Redeemer, the sacrificial Lamb of God, would satisfy all the requirements of the old covenant and make this new covenant possible. Through His servant, Ezekiel, God revealed more details of His plan: "'I will give you a new heart and put a new spirit within you; I will take the heart of stone out of your flesh and give you a heart of flesh. I will put My Spirit within you and cause you to walk in My statutes, and you will keep My judgments and do them. Then you shall dwell in the land that I gave to your fathers; you shall be My people, and I will be your God'" (Ezek. 36:26–28, NKJV).

Through Jeremiah, God promised that He would write His laws on the hearts of His people and that they would know Him as they had never known Him before. Their sins would be forgiven forever (Jer. 31:31–34).

God's Plan Fulfilled

From the heart of God came the fulfillment of His promise to give His people a new covenant. The plan was not new. It was in God's heart from the beginning. From the moment Satan deceived Eve in the garden of Eden and sin entered her heart, God planned the redemption of His people. He would defeat Satan and bring them back into His fellowship. That's why Jesus came. Only a remnant had accepted the old covenant, and only a remnant accepted Jesus when He came as the New Covenant.

In his book, *The Unquiet Ghost: Russians Remember Stalin*, Adam Hochschild ponders the reason why Stalin ranked higher in a recent Russian public opinion poll than did Mikhail Gorbachev. Stalin was responsible for the deaths of at least twenty million Soviet citizens, about one-eighth of the population of the Soviet Union. We wonder why so many admired such a ruler. We search for reasons why millions of people in our century have been so easily persuaded to accept as their leaders Adolf Hitler, Idi Amin, Fidel Castro, Muamar Khaddafi.

Could it be because people admire power? Is that why so few accepted Jesus as their king? He came as a little child, born into a humble family. He worked as a carpenter in the unimportant town of Nazareth. When He began His ministry, He did draw large crowds; but the power of the Godhead that rested in Him—the power of His words, His teaching, His healing, the power He held over life and over death—was not enough for most who heard Him calling, "Come, follow Me." He spoke little of politics, kings, or governments. He did teach about the kingdom of God, but not many were willing to accept a spiritual kingdom over a worldly one. They didn't like God's plan. They wanted a king who would defeat the Romans and take his place on the emperor's throne, a king mighty in battle, in politics, and in power.

When some tried to make Jesus this kind of king, He rejected their plan. He had a plan of His own to bring peace and new life to those living in a world ravaged by sin. Jesus, Son of God, Redeemer, was the supreme and final sacrifice for man's sins—yours and mine. He died on Calvary's cross—for you and for me and for all who would accept Him as the atonement for their sins. When the Son of God arose from the grave, death was defeated. The penalty for our sin was paid.

We can never fully understand the depth of God's love for us. Not many of us would have the courage to die for someone else or to give our child to die in the place of another, but perhaps Sergeant Franciszek Gajowniczek of the defeated Polish army has a better understanding. In July 1941, the sergeant stood at attention and heard the camp deputy commander at Auschwitz shout, "A prisoner has escaped from Block 14. For every man who escapes, ten will die!" A few moments later Sergeant Gajowniczek heard his number called as one of the ten. Number 5659. He stepped forward trembling. He had lived for the day when he would be free to return to his wife and children. He knew the Allies had landed on the shores of France. The war would soon be over. Now he knew he would never see his loved ones again. All hope was gone.

As these thoughts raced through Sergeant Gajowniczek's mind, Father Maximilian Kolbe, a Catholic priest, stepped forward and said to the commandant, "I want to die for this man." Stunned by what he heard, Sergeant Gajowniczek was unable to speak. He knew Father Kolbe to be good and gentle. Perhaps he would die for a close friend, but why should he die for someone he hardly knew?

After the war Sergeant Gajowniczek was released from prison and has traveled the world telling what Father Kolbe did for him. "I have to tell the story," he says. "I was sentenced to die. He gave me back my life."[2]

That's what Jesus did for us.

We still must live in an insecure, war-torn world. Daily, we must listen to those who believe that technology—which offers us fiber optics, electronic libraries, and multiple video channels—will in time bring the answer to our problems. Many will try to convince us that bioethics—organ transplants, euthanasia, and genetic engineering—will bring a more orderly world. Others will search for permanent solutions to the problems of toxic chemicals and hazardous wastes, economic problems or falling stock markets, and failing education; but alone we cannot change the world. Alone we cannot ~~can~~ stop the floods, rid the world of famine, or bring an end to all wars. Neither can we develop a plan that assures us of eternal life, but God can do all these things. He has a plan. He is a covenant God who keeps His promises. His plan was at work when He sent His Son to redeem us, to call us into His family, and to lead us back to the garden. Today He calls us to live within the security of His love. He wants to teach us how to live in the midst of our troubled world.

No, I'll never forget the expression on my Grandma's face. It wasn't a big smile. It was just peaceful, contented, confident. She had so much love in her eyes as she looked at me and then closed them. Her hand squeezed mine ever so gently. I saw her lips move and heard her whisper, "Jesus, Jesus." She was gone. Gone to the One who had called her into His kingdom early in her life and had led her on the right path all her years. Gone to be with Abraham. And King David. And all God's people whom He's taken across that glassy sea, safely to the other side, generation after generation after generation, according to His plan.

Discovering His Plans

1. King David wrote, "As for man, his days are like grass, he flourishes like a flower of the field; the wind blows over it and it is gone, and its place remembers it no more" (Ps. 103:15–16). What thoughts come to your mind as you think about these words?

2. God said, "Let us make man in our image, in our likeness" (Gen. 1:26). What do these words mean to you?

3. Describe a time and place in your life when you felt especially close to God. Why do you think this was so?

4. Why do you think Adam and Eve chose to believe Satan and reject God's Word? What are some of the reasons humans today reject God's Word?

3

His Call

Fifty-nine million newspapers reach American homes daily. Sixty-two million Sunday editions hit the streets weekly.[1] Ninety-eight percent of American homes have at least one television set. A single fiber optic strand can transmit 16,000 telephone conversations at once. *Encyclopaedia Britannica* and the Bible combined can be sent around the world via fiber cable in less than two seconds! A collection of 10,000 volumes will soon be within instant access of anyone with a personal computer.[2]

Messages! Messages! Messages! Today we are bombarded with messages inviting us to respond. Not all are important. Some are. A few are heeded. Others ignored.

We hear: Drive safely. But more than 42,000 people die in car accidents annually, and more than two million are disabled.[3]

We hear: Don't break the law—don't rob people, steal, destroy property, or kill—but more than 948,000 people are in prison in the United States today.[4]

We hear: "To you has been given the secret of the kingdom of God," and everyone who hears the Word of God must respond.

The God who created the world and made us has always had a plan—for the world and for us. Lesslie Newbigin writes that faith in the power of His plan makes it possible "to find meaning for world history which does not make personal history meaningless, and meaning for personal history which does not make world history meaningless."[5] If this is true, then learning about God's plan should be a top priority for all nations and peoples, yet not everyone wants to know about God's plan. Not everyone is interested. Only a few ask questions.

This has always been true. God's plan for Adam and Eve was no secret, but they responded, "No, we will not obey." God explained His plan to Noah, to Abraham and his descendants, to Moses, the Israelites, and the prophets. They all heard, and a remnant in every generation responded, "Yes! We will accept Your covenant, God. We will follow Your plan." But most people responded negatively. They chose to follow a plan of their own. Regardless of the response, the plan moved forward. God was determined to build His kingdom, His family.

In the first century A.D., one young man, son of a Jewish mother and a Gentile father, must have wondered what God was doing. At least we know that he searched for answers to some important questions; he heard a message about God's plan to build a kingdom that he never forgot. An itinerant Rabbi talked about "the secret of the kingdom," although He freely gave the secret to all who would listen. Young Mark listened, and he remembered it in such detail that he wrote it down years later. It was eventually printed in a book that bears his name.

I suppose it's possible that young Mark got the message about the parable of the sower from an older man named Peter, who became his close friend. I like to think Mark himself was among the crowd sitting on the banks of the Sea of Galilee, waiting on the Rabbi to speak. The Rabbi's name was Jesus—Jesus of Nazareth. The people watched as He got into a boat, and some men pushed it out away from shore but left it close enough that all could hear Him.

Let me take you back in time. Picture young Mark sitting quietly on the grassy slope leading down to the Sea of Galilee, waiting for the Rabbi to speak. The bright sun glistens on the water, and Mark shades his eyes with his hand so he can see Peter, the big fisherman, the man who left everything to follow Jesus.

There's something about this Rabbi that draws men to him. Is it His eyes? His voice? He's a powerful Teacher. People say He knows more than the teachers of the Law, and everyone talks about those He has healed—the sick, the lame. The most amazing thing is that incident in the synagogue at Capernaum. People say Jesus spoke with such authority that an evil spirit came out of a tormented man. Authority over the mind, the body, and the spirit. Yes, Jesus of Nazareth has authority. Who can deny it?

Mark remembers a recent incident that incurred the wrath of the teachers of the Law. You see, Jesus had not only healed a paralytic, but He had also forgiven the man's sins. It was Jesus' way of announcing that He was God— the only One the Jews knew could forgive sins. Jesus is God? The uproar among the Pharisees is the talk of the crowd gathered to hear what Jesus will say to their accusations. Do these leaders of the synagogue really believe that this gentle, kind Rabbi is possessed by Beelzebub? Or is it possible that Jesus is indeed the promised Messiah? He does wonderful things. He has great authority. Can it be true?

Look! Jesus is holding up His hands. A hush settles over the crowd. He's about to speak. Let's join Mark and see what the Rabbi has to say.

Hear the Message

"Listen! A farmer went out to sow his seed. As he was scattering the seed, some fell along the path, and the birds came and ate it up. Some fell on rocky places where it did not have much soil. It sprang up quickly, because the soil was shallow. But when the sun came up, the plants were scorched, and they withered because they had no root. Other seed fell among thorns, which grew up and choked the plants, so that they did not bear grain. Still other seed fell on good soil. It came up, grew and produced a crop, multiplying thirty, sixty, or even a hundred times. . . . He who has ears to hear, let him hear." (Mark 4:3–9)

What does the crowd think of the story? Many have come a long way to hear this Rabbi. Was it worth their time? A mother sitting nearby with two children says to them, "That was a nice story! Remember it so you can tell your papa." A man pushes himself to his feet with a walking cane and starts ambling off mumbling, "I came to hear a good theological discussion, but this fellow tells children's stories."

Another man looks thoughtful as he turns to his companion, "This Rabbi is saying more than appears on the surface, you can be sure of that, but I don't have time to figure it out. Look! He's studying the faces of the crowd to see if anyone understands His message." After a few minutes the two men get up and head toward the village. "We'll come back and hear him another day," one says to the other. "We've got more important things to do today."

At least everyone was listening. They heard. That's good. Did you notice that Jesus began with the word "Listen!" and closed with the word "hear"! Every good Jew knows that signals an important message—one worth hearing.

Ask Questions

A few people close to Jesus ask Him what the parable means. Mark moves closer. So do the disciples. Listen! "'The secret of the kingdom of God has been given to you.' But to those on the outside, everything is said in parables.'" What secret is He talking about? And what is the kingdom of God? This secret must be important if He gave it to His disciples—and a few others. Jesus is a divider of people all right. Some people have the secret and others don't. Some are on the "inside"; others are on the "outside." I don't want to be on the outside! Do you? Mark is standing nearby. Let's ask him if he heard the secret.

"I'm not sure if I have it right," Mark says. "That's why I'm here: to find out more. Just listen! He's going to explain the parable."

"Don't you understand this parable? How then will you understand any parable? The farmer sows the word. Some people are like seed along the path, where the word is sown. As soon as they hear it, Satan comes and takes away the word that was sown in them. Others, like seed sown on rocky places, hear the word and at once receive it with joy. But since they have no root, they last only a short time. When trouble or persecution comes because of the word, they quickly fall away. Still others, like seed sown among thorns, hear the word; but the worries of this life, the deceitfulness of wealth and the desires for other things come in and choke the word, making it unfruitful. Others, like seed sown on good soil, hear the word, accept it, and produce a crop—thirty, sixty or even a hundred times what was sown." (Mark 4:13–20)

Had we really been there with Mark, sitting on the grass by the Sea of Galilee, listening to Jesus explain the parable of the sower, I hope we would have seen the love in the Rabbi's eyes and heard the gentleness in His voice. I hope we would have understood that He was pleading for us to understand. "'Don't you understand this parable?'" He asked. "'How then will you understand any parable?'"

Jesus used many parables in His teaching. Seventy are recorded in the Four Gospels. He indicated that the parable of the sower was the key to understanding all of them. Why? Because it is the key to His plan, the key to getting into the kingdom of God; and building a kingdom is His plan.

Let's take a closer look at the explanation Jesus gave. He divided people into four groups, and in several ways the four groups are alike. In each group we find a farmer, seed, and soil. Jesus made it clear that He was the farmer, sowing the Word in people's hearts. He did this in all four groups of people, and they all heard. That's good.

But there the similarities end. A war was going on, and Satan was involved. Although Jesus called all who heard the Word to respond appropriately, not all people did. Let's see how each group responded.

Group One

"The farmer sows the word. Some people are like seed along the path, where the word is sown. As soon as they hear it, Satan comes and takes away the word that was sown in them."

Ever seen this happen? The whole crowd heard the parable when Jesus told it there on the Sea of Galilee. Some thought it was an interesting story, nothing more. Others walked away. They were not interested.

People haven't changed. Today, God's Word is available in almost every language of the world. The majority of people now living on the earth have heard the Word. Many see it as interesting history. Others say it's only myth. Most are too busy to listen. They turn away and refuse to believe.

They're like my friend Harold. Living in the United States, he must have heard God's plan to build His

Kingdom over and over again—even if he never entered a church. But one time Harold went to hear a former Vietnam prisoner of war speak at Vandenberg Air Force Base. He heard a message he didn't expect. The speaker told how God had sustained him during his years of imprisonment and how he had been strengthened and encouraged by Scriptures he had memorized as a child. He said that knowing God more and more was the most important goal in his life and that God wanted each of us to know Him personally. That was the message. Harold heard it, but he didn't like it. He came away angry, and the Word was quickly taken away.

An air force chaplain once told me that he visited a man in the hospital who knew he only had a few hours to live. He was dying and didn't know God. The chaplain said to the man, "I want to tell you about Jesus who loves you and wants to walk with you through this valley." But the man stopped him abruptly and said, "I've heard about Him all my life, and I don't want to hear His name again—not one more time!"

This group hears, but Satan quickly takes away the Word, and they respond: "No!"

Group Two

"Others, like seed sown on rocky places, hear the word and at once receive it with joy. But since they have no root, they last only a short time. When trouble or persecution comes because of the word, they quickly fall away."

We can all think of friends who heard the message, were excited about their new life for a short time, and then fell by the wayside. I remember a young couple who asked Jesus to come into their lives after they had been married for fifteen years. They served God faithfully for several years—even sold their home and moved to Hawaii to receive YWAM (Youth with a Mission) training. But when they returned, they couldn't seem to find a place of service in the church. They wanted to go to the mission field—anywhere. When the pastor asked them to wait a year, they grew impatient. Soon their marriage fell apart. Their son got into drugs. Today, no one knows where Ellen is, and Robert will not see anyone from the church. Were their roots not strong enough? Did we as the church fail them?

Not all of our churches have strong education and discipleship programs. Yet believers need to be taught what it means to be a follower of Jesus Christ. We need to be rooted and grounded in God's Word. Jesus is our example. He taught His disciples daily for three years. He taught them to hear God's voice, to listen carefully, and to obey.

Dr. John Stott, eminent English theologian, was one of the teachers at Regent College in Vancouver one summer when I was there. When he arrived, he was taken to a lovely apartment which had been reserved for him. It provided privacy and quiet, but Dr. Stott immediately asked that a student share the apartment with him. The young man chosen was thrilled to be Dr. Stott's close companion for the summer. Later, Dr. Stott explained that the man who brought him to Christ never missed an opportunity to be with him, to teach him, and to disciple him for five years. Ever since, he had followed the example of his mentor. Now Dr. Stott's young friend would put down deeper roots, and he would come to know God more intimately by spending special time with this godly man.

Many years ago when I served as director of adult ministries at our church, God kept bringing Hosea 4:6 to my mind, again and again: "'My people are destroyed for lack of knowledge'" (NKJV). The word *knowledge* in our Bible means more than an accumulation of facts. Proverbs 9:10 says, "Knowledge of the Holy One is understanding" (NKJV). The Hebrew people saw "knowledge" as active, the entry into a relationship. To "know" God is to enter into an intimate relationship with Him, to accept His love.

Could it be that many people have the facts about God but do not know Him? Could this be why many fall away?

"Since they have no root . . . ." When Jesus was tempted by Satan, He fought with the Word of God. We need to put our roots down deep into God's Word to build a strong foundation. I was surprised when I read in the Barna Report, *What Americans Believe*, that only 12 percent of the Christians surveyed read their Bibles daily. Even more surprising is the report that more than one-third of those who regularly attend church do not read the Bible at all. No roots. "When trouble or persecution comes because of the word, they quickly fall away."

Group Three

"Still others, like seed sown among thorns, hear the word; but the worries of this life, the deceitfulness of wealth and the desires for other things come in and choke the word, making it unfruitful."

Choices. That's what this group is all about. A wonderful pastor and his wife, good friends of ours, just spent a few days in our home. Phil was not brought up in a Christian home, but he came to know the Lord while involved in gang activities on the streets of Los Angeles. His faith never wavers. He knows Jesus is the answer to the concerns of the affluent congregation he pastors. "But," he said, "there are so many things which draw my people away. A golf meet. A boat race. A business meeting. If any of these come up on Sunday, they're not in church. Finances of the church? We're hardly making it. I've preached again and again on tithing, but they don't give." The seed sown among thorns. Choices. Priorities.

Paul Stevens, coauthor with Michael Green of a book titled *New Testament Spirituality*, described the deceitfulness of wealth as "an especially deep test of our faith." He said, "For every ten people that can thrive spiritually in the face of adversity, only one can stand in the face of prosperity."[6] How true.

During the years we lived in military housing all over the country, I collected floor plans, pictures of windows, entry ways, kitchens, closets and all those things that I hoped to someday weave into the house of my dreams. That day did come. We built our new home and moved in. I loved the house. I was proud of it. I never wanted to leave it, but shortly after we moved in, I began to feel uneasy. Was I too attached to the house? True, I kept wanting more and more "things" to put in it, and it was taking more and more of my time and attention.

Then one day a man named Yeng Yang, who had come to our country from Laos, was helping us with some yard work and asked to see the inside of our house. He came in with muddy shoes and left his tracks on my new carpet—across the dining room, into the living room, and down the hallway. I tried not to show how upset I was, but after he left the Lord spoke to me. "Why are you acting as if Yeng Yang is not welcome in this house?" He asked. "Didn't I give it to you that you might use it for the ministry to which I have called you?"

When the Lord finally got through to me, the family gathered and we gave the house back to the Lord. We're His tenants. Over the years, our home has been a refuge for many college students, InterVarsity conferences, and Bible studies. The Lord sends us many guests. At times I have to remind myself that this house is temporary, but how we use it can bring eternal rewards.

Homes, money, business, even travel, education, church activities—anything that takes top priority over God's call upon our lives can become thorns and choke out His Word, His plan for us.

Group Four

"Others, like seed sown on good soil, hear the word, accept it, and produce a crop—thirty, sixty or even a hundred times what was sown."

This is the group I want to be in. Don't you? They hear, accept, and produce. It's interesting that Jesus followed His explanation of the parable with three illustrations of what the kingdom of God is like. Every one of them is about producing, about growth. The first is about a lamp that should be placed on a stand—not under a bowl or under the bed. Jesus said the lamp's light was never meant to be hidden. The second is about seed that is scattered and grows in stages—first the stalk, then the head, and then the full kernel. The third is about the tiny mustard seed that grows and becomes the largest of all the garden plants. Its branches are so big that they can provide shelter for birds to rest in the shade. Yes, the last group in the parable of the sower are people who both grow themselves and produce other believers.

But Jesus gave a warning: "'Consider carefully what you hear, . . . With the measure you use, it will be measured to you—and even more. Whoever has will be given more; whoever does not have, even what he has will be taken from him'" (Mark 4:24–25).

I call this "measure for measure." The Word is never neutral. It brings blessings when accepted. It brings judgment when rejected. As we hear, ask, and obey, we will be given more and more understanding and fruit; but if we neglect the Word we hear, it will be taken from us.

During the five years we lived in El Paso, Texas, I worked hard to learn the Spanish language. I took courses. I read books in Spanish. I welcomed every opportunity to practice with someone who spoke the language well. Finally I reached a level of proficiency that allowed me to interpret for others. Then from El Paso we moved to Maine and then to Montana, and I did not have occasion to speak Spanish. As the years passed, I lost my use of the language. That which we neglect, we lose. It is measure for measure.

Have you ever wondered if those in group three—those caught up in the worries and deceitfulness of the world—could move into group four? I have. The answer is yes. We have examples all around us. Perhaps we were in this group at one time ourselves. To move into group four and to continue to grow as followers of Jesus, we must not only *hear* the Word and *ask* the Spirit to teach us from the Word; we must *obey*.

Obey the Word

Let's go back to the secret of the kingdom that Jesus said had been given to those who asked. Mark found out the secret all right. Later he recorded it in his book: "Then he looked at those seated in a circle around him and said, 'Here are my mother and my brothers! Whoever does God's will is my brother and sister and mother'" (Mark 3:34).

Someone had just told Jesus that His mother and brothers had arrived; He, however, was thinking of a different kind of family, not a family bound by flesh but a family bound by the Spirit. Those who were close to Him, hearing, asking, and doing God's will—these, He said, were His family. That's the secret of His plan. The kingdom of God is the family of God, and we open the door to the kingdom when we *hear*, *ask*, and *obey*.

It's not too hard to hear. It's not hard to ask questions if we're the least bit interested. It's not hard to ask Jesus to be our Redeemer and bring us into His kingdom. But doing God's will? Obeying? That should keep us in God's Word. Clearly, His will is for us to grow as believers—to grow in all the fruits of the Spirit we read about in Galatians 5:22—love, joy, peace, patience, kindness, goodness, faithfulness, gentleness, and self-control. His plan is that we find our place of service in His kingdom, a place of ministry. We will discover dozens of things that are God's will as we read His Word. That's why He gave it to us.

The message Jesus gave on the shores of the Sea of Galilee when He told the parable of the sower is a vitally important message. He revealed the secret of the kingdom of God that day, and He invited all who would like to be a part of His family to respond. That's His call and that's God's plan: to bring His wandering children back into His family, back into His kingdom, the kingdom of God.

Discovering His Plans

1. Make a list of five messages from the secular world that you have heard recently. Check those you consider important. Now list five messages from the Word of God that come to your mind. Of the ten messages, circle the one you believe is the most important to you. Why?

2. In what way is the parable of the sower an important message for you?

3. What is the secret to the kingdom of God—the key that opens the door?

4. Think about the four groups that represent the ways in which people respond to the message of the Word. In which group do you place yourself? Do you know people in each of the four groups? If so, describe their responses to God's important message.

5. List three ways you can help move others from the first three groups to group four.

4

Our Choice

My daughter is a USAF pilot, and once when I was writing a book about her, she arranged for me to have a flight in a simulator at Williams Air Force Base. The flight simulator was the same size as the F-16 and was enclosed so that no light could penetrate. Technology imitated the takeoff, flight, and landing so perfectly that I was sure we were in the air.

Then the lights went out. We were in total darkness, but my daughter knew where to find the light. "Just take my hand," she said. "Hold tight. I'll lead you out." And she did. As she opened the door of the simulator, the light flooded in, and the darkness disappeared.

That's what God does for us. He calls us out of the darkness of sin, hopelessness, and frustration. He leads us into His light, His kingdom, where there is peace, hope, and security. That's His plan.

Jesus demonstrated this truth when a man who was born blind was brought to Him to be healed. Jesus said, "'As long as I am in the world, I am the light of the world.'" Then He made clay with saliva, anointed the eyes of the blind man with the clay, and instantly restored his sight (John 9:1–6, NKJV). On another occasion, Jesus came upon a demoniac who lived in the darkness of a cave. The man had often been bound with shackles and chains, but now no one could bind him because the demons inside him had such strong control over him. To this man bound by darkness in his body, mind, and spirit, Jesus brought healing and freedom and light (Mark 5:1–15).

One more illustration: Jesus had a friend named Lazarus who had been dead four days—dead and buried in a dark tomb with a stone covering the door. Jesus ordered the stone taken away and called, "'Lazarus, come forth!'" (John 11:43, NKJV). Immediately Lazarus came out of the darkness into the light—from death to life. Jesus loved that blind man. He loved the demoniac. He loved Lazarus, and He loves you and me.

Do you remember when Jesus first called you out of darkness into His light? When you knew for sure that He loved you? When you first understood who He was and what He had done for you? I remember. I was eight years old. It was summertime, and our church had a revival. Chairs were set up on the church lawn. A platform was built for the visiting evangelist and the song director. Lights were strung from tree to tree.

My sister Rita and I were to sing a duet that night, "Count Your Blessings," all four verses. Unfortunately, someone failed to coordinate the program and the congregation sang our selection first—all four verses. Somehow Rita and I got through our duet, but we returned to our seats devastated. As I sat there trying to hold back the tears, God's love surrounded me. It was as if Jesus had wrapped His arms around me. "I love you, and I loved your singing," He whispered. Suddenly I understood that He did.

When the pastor invited those who wanted Jesus to be their Savior and Lord to come to the front, I couldn't wait to go forward. My dad saw me ease out of the pew and followed me down the aisle. He explained to me what asking Jesus to come into my heart meant, but I knew. I knew that He was already there. I had joined His family, and my life would never again be the same.

When We Choose to Answer God's Call

We don't have to be perfect to hear God calling us to come into His family and follow His plan for our lives. We only have to hear and respond to His words: "'Come to Me, all you who labor and are heavy laden, and I will give you rest'" (Matt. 11:28, NKJV). When our lives are turned upside down and we don't know which way to turn, He says, "Come to Me." He offers us rest—rest from concern over all the things we've done wrong and rest from worry over all the things that might happen. He forgives us. He guides us. And He teaches us the things we need to change in our lives as He points us in the right direction.

When we ask, He shows us His plan for our lives. Too often we expect to get the whole plan at once, but Jesus teaches us to trust Him by leading us step by step. Even then we sometimes get off the path He has laid out for us. We don't listen, or we choose to take an enticing detour. Our Lord doesn't take away our free choice.

However, we are not to worry. When we get sidetracked, our good Shepherd is with us to help us find our way back to the right path. He guides those who are in His family if we are willing to obey. After awhile, when we're convinced that His path for us is best, we meet other people along the way who need a bit of encouragement, a word, a helping hand, or a sharing of something we've learned. That's the way it is in a family, and we are the family of God.

Hear. Ask. Obey. That's the key that unlocks the door to the kingdom, the family. It is the key that keeps us going down the right path.

It's helpful to see how God has worked out His plan in other people's lives. God has always had a deep desire to include each member of His family in the work of His master plan, that our lives might be more rewarding and that others might be brought into His kingdom. Let's look at the path He laid out for a young man who lived almost four thousand years ago. Joseph's story is in the Old Testament and fills a large part of the Book of Genesis—chapters 37 and 39 through 50.

When Joseph Chose to Hear, Ask, and Obey

Joseph was seventeen years old when God gave him a dream. He saw himself with his brothers in a field binding sheaves. His sheave stood upright, and his brothers' sheaves bowed down to his. We can't be sure that Joseph understood all that God was trying to tell him, but we get the feeling that he did. He must have liked the idea that someday he would rule over his older brothers, and he couldn't wait to tell them. After all, they hated him because he was their father Jacob's favorite son. Jacob kept the boy by his side and gave him the easy jobs. He even made him a beautiful coat of many colors.

When Joseph shared his dream, the brothers hated him even more. One day Jacob sent Joseph to check on his brothers. They were out in the field tending the sheep. When Joseph arrived, the brothers put him in a pit and then sold him to some Midianite traders. In Egypt, the Midianites sold Joseph to Potiphar, an officer of Pharaoh and captain of the guard. This young dreamer found himself alone among strange people in a strange land.

His Attitude

We might expect Joseph to be filled with rage. At the very least he might have been discouraged about the path his life had taken. He was separated from a father who loved and provided abundantly for him and sent to a strange land as a slave. But we don't hear one word of complaint. Rather, Joseph saw the Lord's hand in all that was happening to him. Look what we are told about him: "The LORD was with Joseph, and he was a successful man; and he was in the house of his master the Egyptian. And his master saw that the LORD was with him and that the LORD made all he did to prosper in his hand" (Gen. 39:2–3, NKJV). Joseph served Potiphar well. He was a hard and honest worker. He obeyed Potiphar, and he obeyed God.

His Rocky Path

There are always temptations along the way. We can take detours if we choose to do so, or we can walk straight down the path of God's plan. Potiphar's wife enticed Joseph and then grew angry when he resisted her advances. She falsely accused this faithful servant, and Potiphar cast him into prison.

Did this cause Joseph to doubt that God had a plan for his life? No. During all the years Joseph spent in prison, he knew the presence of the Lord. "The LORD was with Joseph and showed him mercy, and He gave him favor in the sight of the keeper of the prison. . . . the LORD was with him and; whatever he did, the LORD made it prosper" (Gen. 39:21, 23, NKJV).

One day Joseph saw the despair of the royal butler and baker who had displeased Pharaoh and been thrown into prison. When they told Joseph they could find no one to interpret their dreams, Joseph said, "'Do not interpretations belong to God? Tell them to me, please'" (Gen. 40:8, NKJV).

Joseph was sensitive to God's leading. He knew God would give him the interpretations, and He did. Both men would be released from prison in three days, the baker to be beheaded and the butler to return to Pharaoh's service. Joseph said to the butler, "'Remember me when it is well with you'" (Gen. 40:14, NKJV). However, the butler forgot about Joseph when he was back in the daily grind of things. Perhaps he was ungrateful, or perhaps the timing was not right for God's plan. Either way we might have been discouraged, but not Joseph. He went about his daily tasks and waited.

His Trust in God

Two years passed before Pharaoh had a dream and needed an interpreter. Then the butler remembered Joseph and told Pharaoh about him.

When Joseph was called before Pharaoh, he was confident that God would not fail him. He interpreted Pharaoh's dream to mean that Egypt would have seven years of plenty followed by seven years of famine. Pharaoh was impressed with this young Israelite. So impressed was he that he asked his servant, "'Can we find such a one as this, a man in whom is the Spirit of God?'" (Gen. 41:38, NKJV). Pharaoh made Joseph his right-hand man, second in command over all Egypt. Joseph was only thirty years of age.

Pharaoh also gave Joseph a wife, not an Israelite, but the daughter of an Egyptian priest. We see Joseph's attitude toward the path he was following at this point in his life when his two sons were born: "Joseph called the name of the firstborn Manasseh: 'For God has made me forget all my toil and all my father's house.' And the name of the second he called Ephraim: 'For God has caused me to be fruitful in the land of my affliction'" (Gen. 41:51–52, NKJV).

We might wonder how Joseph, living in a pagan land, was able to follow God's plan for his life so well. **God is** anxious to reveal His plan to those who are willing to hear His voice, to ask for His guidance, and to obey His commands. Joseph was willing. He knew God had a plan for his life, although I doubt if he could ever have imagined the great impact his life would have on God's plan for His kingdom. During the years of plenty, Joseph filled Pharaoh's storehouses with grain. Then when the seven years of famine came, there was bread in Egypt.

His Assurance

Joseph's brothers came to Egypt for bread because the famine was severe in their land. They didn't recognize their younger brother when they bowed down before him and asked for bread. Joseph recognized them; however, he didn't reveal his identity. Perhaps he had a hard time forgiving his brothers for selling him as a slave to be taken to Egypt. That might well have been our response. But more than this, I believe Joseph needed time to fully understand God's plan; and he wanted to bring his brothers to an understanding of that plan.

After three days, Joseph said to his brothers, "'If you are honest men, let one of your brothers stay here in prison, while the rest of you go and take grain back for your starving households. But you must bring your youngest brother to me, so that your words may be verified and that you may not die'" (Gen. 42:19–20). Simeon stayed; the others returned to Jacob with an abundance of grain.

When the brothers were once again in need of grain, they returned to Egypt with Benjamin, the youngest in the family. Joseph kept them in Egypt for some time and tested them by having a silver cup placed in Benjamin's sack when they left. When the cup was discovered by a steward Joseph sent after his brothers, they were all returned to Egypt. Joseph was now ready to reveal his identity. As his brothers stood before him terrified, he said: "'I am your brother Joseph, the one you sold into

Egypt! And now, do not be distressed and do not be angry with yourselves for selling me here, because it was to save lives that God sent me ahead of you. . . . God sent me ahead of you to preserve for you a remnant on earth and to save your lives by a great deliverance'" (Gen. 45:4–5, 7).

When Joseph broke down in tears and embraced his brothers, they were as amazed as we would have been. Pharaoh heard what had happened and said to Joseph, "'Tell your brothers, "Do this: Load your animals and return to the land of Canaan, and bring your father and your families back to me. I will give you the best of the land of Egypt and you can enjoy the fat of the land"'" (Gen. 45:17–18).

All of Jacob's family moved to Egypt according to God's plan. Joseph lived to enjoy his great-grandchildren and died at age 110. He was embalmed and placed in a coffin in Egypt.

What can we learn from Joseph? How can his story help us when we live in such a different world? Let me suggest three things.

First, hear what God is saying. That is what Joseph did. Like Joseph, when something happens to turn our lives in a different direction, we need to listen with an open mind. God will help us understand. He may have a place of service waiting for us in a new job or in a different town. Or, He may have a difficult situation He wants us to deal with on our way to becoming mature believers.

Second, ask God for help. He has warned us to expect temptations, bumps along the way, and crossroads that could lead us in the wrong direction. Joseph had his share of temptations. He had some difficult choices to make, but He trusted God to help him. God will never take away our free will, but He will help us to choose the right way.

Third, obey God. Did you notice how patient Joseph was? He waited for God to work out His plan in His own time. We can walk with that same assurance and peace.

God made us. He knows us perfectly. He will keep His promise to lead us all the way.

When We Need
Encouragement along the Way

We fail, and we need a lot of encouragement. There are times in all our lives when we wonder if God has forgotten us. Then we ask the hard questions. Have you ever spent hours on a project and had it fail? Totally fail? You may have asked God, "How could You stand by and let all my work go down the drain? Don't You care?" Or you may have lost your job, struggled through months of unsuccessful searching for another one, and faced a zero bank balance. You wonder, "Where is God now? Is He going to get me through all this?"

If you think we need answers to these questions, let me tell you about a man named John who was banished by the Roman emperor Domitian to a tiny little island of Patmos. Domitian thought he was more worthy to be worshiped than John's God; however, John would never agree to that. At the time, John was almost a hundred years old. He had white hair and a long, white beard. He walked with a cane, lived in a cave, and spent his days just talking with the Lord. John had every reason to be discouraged as he went through his days alone on this island.

When he was just a young man he left everything— good job, family, and friends—to follow a Jewish Rabbi who had little more than the clothes on His back. John probably couldn't tell us what first drew him to this gentle Rabbi who quietly called him to drop his nets and follow. John was the take-charge type, a boisterous, demanding, rowdy fisherman; but the day came when John recognized Jesus of Nazareth as the promised Messiah. Then he knew he was serving the King of kings. Nothing else mattered.

John was faithful even after his King was taken from him—crucified on a cross.

Later when John saw the risen Lord, he began his crusade. He wanted everyone to know the truth about God and His plan to redeem humankind. John pastored the church at Ephesus where he deeply loved and cared for his people. A special joy for him must have been writing the story of his travels with the Messiah and what he had learned from Him. Since all the other apostles had been martyred, John's biography of Jesus was the last—seasoned with years of living the life of a firm believer.

Then Domitian issued his command: "Send that man to Patmos. Get him out of circulation. Let him worship his God—alone!" That's when I think John asked God the hard questions. That's when he wondered if he was on the right path. That's when he needed some strong words of encouragement.

Can you relate to John? I can. We often need words of encouragement and help when God changes the direction of our lives. Especially is this true when we are satisfied, contented with our lives as they are.

Several years ago I was teaching at a community college near my home. I loved it there. I was teaching literature, which meant that I had to do lots of reading and reading is one of the things I enjoy the most. I sponsored a Christian club on campus and looked forward to going with the students on retreats every fall and spring. The faculty were my friends. I planned to teach at Allan Hancock College the rest of my life.

Then one day my pastor called me into his office. "I need you full-time on my staff," he said. Just like that. Give up my teaching position? Join the church staff at double the hours and half the pay? No way! I made every excuse in the book! But God was there and in time got through to me. When the path of my life was unclear, muddled, and frustrated, He gave me a fresh sense of direction. He reminded me of His plan for my life, and I found joy in that new job. God was with me. I knew I was on the right path. He is a great God. A great Encourager.

That's what God did for John. He gave him a vision that was so magnificent, so splendid, that John would never again be uncertain about God's plan or the path he traveled. God gave John the total picture. He showed John the work He was doing among His people at that very moment, and He mapped out His plan to the end of the story. He is a great God. A great Encourager.

The exciting part is that this vision of God's plan with all the signs and warnings along the way was not just for John. It was meant to encourage you and me. It was a gift to all God's people.

In John's vision, Jesus stood in the midst of His church and said to His servant, "'Write the things which you have seen, and the things which are, and the things which will take place after this'" (Rev. 1:19, NKJV). That's the whole story! The threads of God's covenant plan to redeem His people are woven through the Old Testament books, and His plan is fulfilled through Christ Jesus in the New Testament; but this last book, with letters to His church—you and me—propels us into the future!

Do you understand why God shared all this with us? Why He chose to give us so much encouragement along the journey? Our almighty, powerful God knew our lives would not always be easy. He knew Satan was calling in his troops and planning some major battles—more fierce than God's people had ever experienced before. He knew we needed encouragement to stay on the right path.

With all this encouragement, you'd think we would never take a wrong turn and never wander off the path. Not so. We do.

When We Take
Detours and Lose the Way

The highways in the United States are clearly marked. Even numbered highways run east and west; odd numbered ones run north and south. Federal highway numbers are placed in a shield; state highway numbers are inside a circle. Three numbers indicate a loop or a bypass. Signs every few miles point us in the direction we are going. At times we turn off on a little country road that looks interesting or we decide to take a shortcut, and we get lost. When this happens, we need help!

I have a friend named Kay, an energetic, vivacious, young school counselor who spends her summers hiking in Glacier National Park. Kay knows the country well and understands the need for the signs that warn hikers to stay on the well-marked paths. But one bright sunny day in August she discovered a path that excited her love of adventure; she couldn't resist taking a detour. It was a narrow path, but it showed signs that it had been traveled before. She was alone when she turned and started up the new path, and by noon she noticed that she had climbed to great heights. The path began to get rocky and difficult. At times it almost disappeared. She thought about turning back, but Kay was not a quitter. She was determined to find out what was at the end of the trail. She went on.

By mid-afternoon, when she was struggling to find her way, she saw bear tracks and broken branches—a sure sign of trouble ahead. *What will I do if I meet a grizzly?* she whispered to herself. The sound of each bird call, each leaf that fell, each crunch of the twigs under her feet magnified in the woods. The path was now thick with underbrush, and the trees were so close together that little light was coming through. Looking at her map once again, Kay reasoned that she had gone in a semicircle and was only a few miles from camp. The way ahead would be dangerous, and she wasn't sure she could make it. Should she turn around and try to make her way back to the right path? Or should she go on and hope that her map was right?

It was at that moment, Kay said later, that God's voice came through to her. "Turn back to the right path," God said, "I'll be with you."

"Suddenly I wasn't alone," Kay said, "and I knew I'd make it back to camp." She turned back to a connecting road, moving slowly and cautiously through the dense underbrush. It was hard. At times the path was barely visible, but she kept her eyes and ears open and she knew she wasn't alone. "God was so close to me," Kay said. "I felt safe even with danger all around me." Just before dark settled over the mountains, Kay came back onto the right path and within a short time arrived safely at camp.

When we are tempted and take a detour, we need to remember God's message to Kay: "Turn back to the right path. I'll be with you." He is there when the clouds settle, and we can't see clearly in the darkness. He is there when we come to a crossroad, and we don't know which way to turn. God is our Light. He will lead us back to the right path.

Yes, God had a plan for Joseph. He had a plan for John, and He has a plan for you and for me. It's His plan, but it's our choice.

Discovering His Plans

1. Think about the time you first knew God was calling you to follow Him. Did you *hear* the call? Did you *ask* Jesus to take over your life? Did you promise to *obey* Him?

2. How does Joseph's life encourage you?

3. In what way can you relate to John's experiences of trusting God in difficult times?

4. Recall a time when you took a detour off the path you believe was God's plan for your life. What brought you back to His plan?

5. What are some of the reasons we sometimes choose to detour from God's plan for our lives?

5

Loved by Our Father

The relationship I had with my father shaped my life in many ways. I was the oldest of three daughters, and Dad thought I could do just about anything. Mother was ill during much of my growing up years, and I learned early to care for my younger sisters and make decisions. Since we lived far from school and there were no school buses in those days, Dad taught me to drive. The state of Texas issued me a driver's license. I not only was responsible for driving my sisters and myself to school, but I picked up two of my cousins along the way. I bought groceries, did the household shopping, and managed a budget at age twelve. Dad trusted me to do all these tasks, and I did them faithfully because I wanted to please him. If I was certain of one thing in my life when I was growing up, it was that my father loved me.

I knew that he would forgive me for any mistakes that I made—like the time I had my first car accident. I pulled onto a main street and an oncoming car crushed my front fender—really crushed it. Dad was only a phone call away and he arrived in record time. He ran toward me shouting, "Are you all right? Are you all right?" When he saw I wasn't hurt, only scared, he held me close and said, "Don't worry about the car. It can be repaired. I'm just thankful you weren't hurt." Then he handed me his car keys and said, "You take my car and go on home. I'll take care of things here. We all make mistakes, and I know you've learned from this one."

I always knew I could trust Dad to take care of me. Few of the ranchers in the flatlands of Texas had more problems than my dad during the depression years. Life was not easy, but Dad made sure that we had food on our table—enough to share with anyone who came to our door hungry. The long talks on our front porch in the evenings fed our minds and spirits. My sisters and I learned about our loving heavenly Father from those talks.

I know now that to a large measure my father was responsible for the ease with which I came to join God's family and to accept God as my heavenly Father. That's what God intended—that our human parents reflect His love and nature and that our earthly families be little microcosms of His larger plan, the family of God.

Some of you have fathers like mine, and this makes it easier for us to accept God's love. We can even accept the truth that though our earthly fathers sometimes disappoint us, or fail us, our Heavenly Father never will.

Studies show we're in the minority, however. Not all believers were brought up in loving homes. Not all fathers follow God's plan and model His love. If this is true for you, you may still have a hard time grasping the image of God as a loving Father.

Carol did. She's a friend of mine, the daughter of a couple who belonged to the Sinners, a motorcycle gang in southern California. When Carol was a little girl, she was severely mistreated by her father. Every day he told her that she was a bad girl. He punished her harshly.

Then he molested her—repeatedly. She often stood by helplessly as her father abused her mother.

When Carol was twelve years of age, her father was arrested. She was placed in a Christian foster home. For the first time in her life, Carol knew peace. In that home she learned about God and saw that all families were not like her own. She was deeply loved. Best of all, her foster father taught her about the love of a heavenly Father. *Mr. Hensley is kind and loving*, she thought. *Perhaps this heavenly Father is kind and loving too.* The Hensleys all thought so, but Carol wasn't sure. Unknowingly, she had transferred the characteristics of her own father to her heavenly Father. She saw Him as a selfish, cruel, commander who was never fair, never loving; she was sure she could never please Him. With the help of the Hensleys and a good pastor, Carol gave her life to Jesus and joined His family. But her struggle did not end. She spent years learning to accept love.

Carol married a youth minister, and in time her loving husband and Christian friends helped her to see that God was not like her earthly father at all. God's love spilled over into all her relationships. She and Steve now rear three children in a house filled with God's love.

Our God never changes. He is the same yesterday, today, and forever. He will never stop loving us. The family concept that He planned in the beginning has not always been followed. It is going through a rapid change in the twentieth century. This distorted view of the family has a strong impact on whether we are able to accept God's unconditional love and join His family.

The upheaval in American families is one of the many earthshaking trends that Russell Chandler reviews in his book, *Racing Toward 2001*. One out of four family groups in our nation today are single-parent homes. One third of these single-parent families is headed by a divorced mother, and 28 percent by a never-married mother. By the end of the century these households are expected to grow to thirteen million.[1] Children brought up in homes without a father often have a difficult time understanding the love of God the Father. This is especially true if the father deserted the family or stopped loving them. Would not their heavenly Father do the same? These distorted views of what God is like have negative carryover.

Sometimes our earthly fathers are not the only ones who can cause us to have a distorted view of our heavenly Father. At some time or another, most of us have experienced rejection by classmates or teachers or someone in our church. Repeated rejection can cause us to wonder if anyone loves us—even God. If others reject us, maybe God will too. Consider some possible scenarios:

The first one: Hot sun. Clear day. Quiet street. The neighborhood boys mark off the bases. It's time for baseball. Two boys start choosing teams, calling names. Bobby. Tom. Jack. Billy. . . . One little boy stands in the back digging a hole with the toe of his shoe. He wears a new, bright red baseball cap. He stares at the ground. He never looks up. No one calls Tim. No one wants him.

The second one: Late spring. Rainy day. High school campus. Graduation is two days away. There is a party tomorrow night. One girl is cleaning out her locker. She's average looking, with a pretty face, but she doesn't smile. She hears the happy voices as her classmates pass by. They have dates for the party. No one has asked her—no one. She's never had a date, and she won't be back after today—not for the party, not for graduation.

The third one: Dim lights. Sunday evening. Church election. A tall, straight-faced man stands. He reads the names and number of votes. A quiet, elderly man rises from the back row. He slips out the door unnoticed and trudges home to an empty house. He had hoped he would be elected. What joy to be a deacon! He had the time to give, to serve. But he didn't have an important job or the right clothes. He was a background person who just loved Jesus, a real servant. But he'd never be elected. Not in this church.

Do any of these scenarios bring back memories? Have there been times in your life when you felt no one loved you? But there's good news. People disappoint us. We don't have to accept a distorted view of God gained from our experiences with people. We can know God as He is. God's love will never stop reaching out to us regardless of what our past relationships have been like. He calls us to come into His family. To be His children. That's His desire.

Father to the Israelites

We get some help in knowing our Father from the ancient Israelites—but not much. God's plan was at work. The idea of a family with God as the Father was there. The Israelites knew the concept of *father*. The word is used more than seven hundred times in the Old Testament, but only seven times is *Father* used as a title for God. There was a distance between God and His people. God called them. But they didn't trust Him. They feared Him and did not always obey Him. Just like today, only a remnant understood that their Creator loved them and would always work for their best interests.

Moses understood. "'Is he not your Father, your Creator, who made you and formed you?'" he asked the Israelites (Deut. 32:6). King David understood. Speaking of David's son, Solomon, God said, "'I will be his father, and he will be my son. . . . my love will never be taken away from him'" (2 Sam. 7:14–15).

Again and again over the years, the goodness and mercy of a loving Father is seen as He called to those He loved. "'How gladly would I treat you like sons,'" He said, "'and give you a desirable land, the most beautiful inheritance of any nation.' I thought you would call me 'Father' and not turn away from following me'" (Jer. 3:19). Only when the Israelites were in deep distress would they call out to the only One who could help them. A few were brought to their knees in sincere repentance and said, "O LORD, you are our Father. We are the clay, you are the potter; we are all the work of your hand" (Isa. 64:8). That was the remnant—just a few faithful sons.

But perhaps we shouldn't be too hard on these early Israelites. Their picture of God was incomplete. Those who heard His voice in the thunder and storm trembled. To be truthful, they blamed God for their troubles; and they had their own plans. God's plan to build a family and be their Father was not an easy one for these prideful and headstrong people to accept. Come to think of it, the plan hasn't been easy for people of any age to accept. It's surprising that God didn't give up on us years ago, but He didn't. He sent His Son.

"Abba, Father" to Jesus

In the New Testament, "father" is used 391 times and 248 of these refer to God as "Father"! That's quite a change. What happened?

Jesus came. His vision of the Father was crystal clear. He knew His own relationship with the Father. He knew the relationship the Father wanted with those who would come to Him. And that relationship was not that perceived by the Jews of His day. Jesus called God "Abba, Father"; the Jews never did—never. It was unthinkable. *Abba*, the Aramaic word which translated into Greek as "Father" was used by a child to address his father or a rabbi, but never for the Almighty. *Abba* was an intimate family word. It denoted closeness: And who would dare come close to the Almighty? Then there was the problem of the word *Abba* coming from Aramaic—the every day language of the common people. One of the first words spoken by children of Aramaic speaking parents was *Abba*.

Yet Jesus called God *Abba*. He gave His disciples the authority to do so. No individual in the Old Testament, not one of the leading Jewish religious leaders of Jesus' day, ever addressed God as Father until Jesus came and taught us to say "Abba, Father." The Lord's Prayer begins with *Abba*. We use the word *dad* or *daddy* today in the same way. It is a tender, loving, caring word. Our Abba, Father.

Did you ever know someone with great authority, someone whom you highly respected, who asked you to call him by his first name? I respected Dr. Ralph Wardell not only because of his wisdom, but also because of his genuine fairness and concern for others. He was my English professor. One day after I graduated from college and started teaching under his direction, he asked me to call him by his first name. I was honored. I had no less respect for him. I still held him in the same high regard, but by having the privilege of using his first name our relationship changed. It was warmer, more intimate. Was that not what Jesus wanted to teach us about our Father?

We can understand how deep the Father's love was for us by noting Jesus' relationship to the Father in the garden of Gethsemane and on the cross. "'Abba, Father,'" He said, "'everything is possible for you. Take this cup from me. Yet not what I will, but what you will'" (Mark 14:36). Yes, their relationship was close. Father and Son. But the cup remained. The Father and the Son carried out their plan willingly.

While hanging on the cross, Jesus cried out in Aramaic, "'My God, my God, why have you forsaken me?'" Not "Abba, Father," but "My God, my God." God turned His back on His Son that He might pay the price for our sins—yours and mine. The separation from God—the Son from Abba, Father—was the torment far greater than the physical suffering of the cross. It was the only way our rejection of God could be forgiven and we could be saved from the eternal torment of separation from God. When

Jesus rose from the grave, the penalty for our sin was paid. Death was defeated.

That's how much God loves us. He gave His only Son that we might be brought into His family and that we might have the privilege of calling Him "Abba, Father."

Not "Father" to Everyone

The prophet Malachi asked some important questions: "Have we not all one Father? Did not one God create us?" (2:10). And five hundred years later Paul wrote, "For this cause I bow my knees unto the Father of our Lord Jesus Christ, of whom the whole family in heaven and earth is named" (Eph. 3:14–15, KJV). True. God is the Father of all creation. He planned it. He started the family, but God is *not* the father of every person in the spiritual sense. That's what counts—for all eternity.

How do we know this? Jesus said so. He made it clear that there is a difference between physical "descendants" and "spiritual children." The Jews had great pride in calling Abraham their father. One day they were bragging about this to Jesus who said to them, "'I know you are Abraham's descendants.'" Then He made His point: "'If you were Abraham's children, then you would do the things Abraham did.'" They were *descendants* but not children. He was Creator but not their Father. The Jews became angry. "'We are not illegitimate children,'" they protested. "'The only Father we have is God himself'" (John 8:37, 39, 41). Not so. Jesus didn't let this statement pass unchallenged.

Look how He set them straight: "'If God were your Father, you would love me, for I came from God and now am here. I have not come on my own; but he sent me. Why is my language not clear to you? Because you are unable to hear what I say. You belong to your father, the devil, . . . He who belongs to God hears what God says.

The reason you do not hear is that you do not belong to God'" (John 8:42–44, 47).

Jesus clearly abolished the idea of the universal fatherhood of God. Either God is our Father or Satan is. That's the choice.

"Abba, Father" to Believers

In a special sense, God is the Father of believers—those who have trusted Jesus as Savior and have received eternal life. This isn't based on natural birth. Jesus said, "I tell you the truth, no one can see the kingdom of God unless he is born again" (John 3:3). The second birth is spiritual. Jesus came that we might have a new birth, a new life. Remember what He said? "'I am the way, the truth, and the life. No one comes to the Father except through Me'" (John 14:6, NKJV). Yes, He's the way—the way into the family of God, the way back to Abba, Father.

I have a niece who has adopted two children—a girl and a boy. These children were not born to Beth and Bill naturally. They were rescued from lives of poverty and deprivation. They were chosen and brought into Beth and Bill's family. They were given their adopted father's name. They are loved and cherished and protected. Always they are guided and disciplined that they may grow up to be all that their parents hope and plan for them. Now they have a whole family of relatives to enjoy—grandparents, aunts, uncles, and cousins. They are also the heirs of the family inheritance.

What Beth and Bill have done for Penny and Chris is what God has done for us—and more. He has rescued us from eternal darkness, saved us from eternal punishment, and brought us into His family (Acts 26:18). He has given us a new name (Rev. 3:12). He loves us, protects us, and disciplines us (Rev. 3:19). We enjoy the fellowship of a whole family of believers (1 John 1:7), and we have a glorious inheritance waiting for us (1 Pet. 1:3–4).

Those of us who were brought up in loving Christian homes sometimes find it hard to comprehend all that Jesus has done for us. We can easily be guilty of taking His sacrifice on the cross for granted. Sometimes God has to call us to Himself and remind us that we must be more than "descendants" of Christian parents. We must all be born again spiritually. We must individually make the choice to come to the Father through Jesus. Only Jesus Christ is the "only begotten Son" of the Father. We must be adopted. But no matter what our background, we all begin a new life from that moment when we come into His kingdom, His family. That's our Father's plan.

The joy of adoption, the joy of having God as our Father, far exceeds any other joy we can imagine. No wonder Paul included "our Father" and "Jesus our Lord" in the greeting of every letter he wrote to the churches. He knew the joy of being in the family of God. Paul knew that he had come into the family through Jesus and could now call "Abba, Father." And so can you and I.

Discovering His Plans

1. What three words best describe your earthly father?

2. In what way have your experiences with your earthly father affected your relationship with your heavenly Father?

3. Most of us have experienced rejection at some time in our lives—as children and as adults. If this is true for you, how did being rejected make you feel? What evidence do you have that your heavenly Father will never fail you?

4. What is the difference between "descendants" and "spiritual children," as Jesus explained the terms?

5. Explain John 3:3. "I tell you the truth, no one can see the kingdom of God unless he is born again."

Part 2
The Nature of His Call

6

Called to Be Like Jesus

When we were growing up, I suspect each of us at one time or another was told, "You're just like your mother!" or "You're just like your father!" We take on family characteristics, ways of thinking and doing things, because we spend so much time together.

God's plan for us, as members of His family, is that we become like His Son. Jesus came to be our Savior and our Lord, but He also modeled the kind of person we are to become. Peter wrote that we are to follow "in his steps" (1 Pet. 2:21). We are called to be like Jesus.

I remember when I registered for practice teaching, Education 304. I was excited. At last, I thought, I would stand before thirty-five enthusiastic students and really teach. As a child, I gathered the neighborhood children in our backyard to play school, and I was always the teacher. Now as an eager college student I pictured myself before a class of my own within a week. I planned to teach those students all I had learned in college—and in my eighteen years of living. I was ready.

I'm sure you know that this isn't what happens in Education 304. "Just sit on the back row so the students won't know you're here," my instructor said. "You observe. Listen. Watch me." Not once during those first few weeks was I allowed to get before the class. I observed. I listened. I focused on Mrs. Allison's every word, every action.

The second semester I often found myself at the front of the room, but Mrs. Allison stayed close by. She encouraged me, corrected me, and saved me from many embarrassing situations. I quickly recalled ways she had handled problems in the classroom; more and more I found myself using her teaching methods.

One day a student in the class remarked, "You're becoming so much like Mrs. Allison that when I'm listening to you I forget she's not teaching." What a compliment to me!

That's God's plan for us: "to be conformed to the likeness of his Son" (Rom. 8:29). He wants us to become so much like Jesus that as we live out our lives in our homes, in the workplace, and in our church, others will see His likeness in us and desire to know Him.

Called to Follow in His Footsteps

The Book of Mark in our Bibles is a great training manual. Observing Jesus as He trained the disciples can teach us in many ways. In chapter 1, Jesus issued a call: "'Come, follow me.'" We might wonder why Peter, Andrew, James, and John were so quick to follow. They were fishermen with work to do. They had families. Why should they follow this stranger from Galilee? Perhaps it was the confidence they saw in His face that drew them or the sense of mission or the love. They must have seen all these in Jesus—in His face, in His voice, in the movement of His hand as He bid them, "Come, follow me."

When we read how quickly the disciples answered the call of Jesus, we wonder why we are so slow to obey. We hesitate. We question. We rationalize.

For three years Jesus walked before these disciples, His family, doing all the things He wanted them to learn. He taught them how to live and how to do the tasks He did. Always He held them accountable. As they heard His teaching, asked questions, and obeyed His instructions, they became more and more like Jesus. Later, their lives reflected His likeness, and others were drawn into His family.

That's God's plan for us. It is a big order, but He is a big God. He has made a way. We can do what the disciples did. We can observe Him, listen to Him, and do our best to imitate Him. We have His Word.

We must not get discouraged. We all know "super-saints" who are closer to being like Jesus than we imagine we'll ever be, but they are just a little farther down the same road we travel. And they can be an encouragement to us.

If we are to become like Jesus, we must keep our eyes on Him. We're in a lifetime learning process; however, at the moment, as we look in the Word and observe Him, you may see something different from what I see. We don't all grow in the same way or have the same needs at the same time, but there are five characteristics none of us can afford to miss. You can work on others later.

Goal Oriented

Jesus was focused on a goal. That's important. Today, people change their goals frequently. I have a twelve-year-old friend who at one time was sure he wanted to be a helicopter pilot. Then he got interested in taking pictures and decided he'd be a photographer. Before long he decided he'd develop his artistic talent and become an artist. Today he is sure he'll be a mechanic because he enjoys helping his dad work on their car.

What about Jesus? He could have focused on being a carpenter. He was well trained. He could have become a famous rabbi and gained recognition in the religious community. No rabbi had more knowledge. Or He could have led a rebellion against the Romans. He was King of kings. He didn't focus on any of these—not as a life goal.

At age twelve Jesus knew what His primary purpose was. He knew His life's goal. That year, He went with His parents to Jerusalem to celebrate the Passover feast. Jesus became separated from Mary and Joseph, and when they found Him, He was in the temple teaching the religious scholars—teaching them! Then Jesus asked his mother, "'Why did you seek Me? Did you not know that I must be about My Father's business?'" (Luke 2:49, NKJV). His goal was fixed and unchangeable. He would carry out His Father's plan, and it was top priority.

We need that sense of mission, that focused goal: to become more like Jesus and to participate in His plan. We may move in many different circles, live in different places, and work at different jobs. Jesus did. But behind all the priorities of our lives is His primary goal for us: We are to become more like the One we choose to follow.

I doubt that the disciples were focused on this goal when they answered Jesus' call. No, becoming like Jesus wasn't exactly what they had in mind. There were a lot of interesting things to do in the Roman world, and these were ambitious men. After they were with Jesus for awhile, He threw them a hard question which must have halted their speculations—at least for the moment. "What good is it," He asked, "for a man to gain the whole world, yet forfeit his soul?" Now that requires some thought.

Years ago a seminar leader asked us to draw a line across a sheet of paper. "Now imagine," he said, "that the line keeps going to your left on and on and on until it is out of sight. Then, imagine the line on your right extends far, far beyond your vision. Next put a cross on the line to mark the time Jesus came into the world. Then a dot when you were born. Last, place a dot on the line to mark the date you will leave this earth."

That seminar leader got my attention. We don't have much time. Every day counts. I want the goal for my life to be focused. I want to be like Jesus, and I want to carry out His plan for my life. What about you?

Patient

Jesus was patient. I'm not a very patient person. If I had written the song, "Make Me Like You, Lord," I would probably have added the word *Now!* Once I get an idea in my head, I often charge ahead, anxious to see the finished result. I've had to struggle over the years to be patient with others who don't always move at the same pace. But patience is something Jesus wants us to learn.

I know this because Jesus was patient. As we follow the twelve disciples through the pages of Mark's Gospel, we wonder why Jesus chose them. They argued. They were selfish. They misunderstood everything Jesus tried to teach them. I'm not sure they ever learned anything the first time around. They certainly didn't understand His plan. When Jesus called them, the disciples were not very much like Him, but they had a patient teacher.

Remember when Jesus fed the five thousand? The story is in Mark 6. The point was not just to satisfy those hungry people. He was teaching and training the disciples. When evening came and the people were hungry, all the disciples could suggest was, "'Send the people away so they can go to the surrounding countryside and villages and buy themselves something to eat'" (v. 36). Let them buy their own food. It was the wrong solution to the problem. "'You give them something to eat,'" Jesus said.

They were shocked! Food costs money. How could they feed so many people? Impossible! How earnestly Jesus wanted them to know who He was, why He had come, and why He had called them. Patiently He gave directions, included the disciples in the task, and fed the people.

However, that's not the end of the story. Turn to Mark 8. Why do you think Jesus fed four thousand people a short time afterward? It was a repeated lesson patiently taught. Then Jesus tested His students with questions and answers. Yet they still did not understand.

I imagine Jesus must have thought, *How can I get through to these men? They mean well, but they don't understand. I have to find another way—get them to think beyond the physical to spiritual things, get them to see clearly who I am.* Just at that moment some people brought a blind man to Jesus and asked that He heal him. No big task. Jesus had healed many blind men before. He could have said, "Be healed," and the man's sight would have been restored instantly. But He didn't.

The disciples watched. First, Jesus touched the man's eyes and asked, "'Do you see anything?'" Yes, he saw people who looked like trees. The man was close to Jesus, standing right in front of Him, but he looked away and didn't see Him. Jesus put His hands on the man's eyes once again. This time his sight was restored, and he saw everything clearly. Did the disciples understand that their vision like the blind man's was distorted? Was the lesson over? No.

Only after all this teaching could Jesus get to the heart of the matter. Only then were the disciples ready. He approached the big question with another: "'Who do people say I am?'" They had the answer to that one. Then, "'But what about you?' he asked. 'Who do you say I am?'" Peter knew. "'You are the Christ.'"

Does seeing Jesus' patience with these disciples encourage you? It does me. I know He won't give up on me when I'm struggling to learn patience myself. It takes patience to teach children to pick up their clothes. I like an orderly room. That means coats hung in the closet, socks and underwear arranged neatly in a drawer, dirty clothes in the laundry basket, school books on the desk. Is that too much to ask?

It takes patience to wait on God to answer my prayers. I know His promises. I know He hears me when I pray. But why does it takes so long to get an answer? If you're like me, you don't always like the waiting period. He has never failed me. The answer always comes. But I know I need to learn more patience if I want to be like Jesus. And I do.

Compassionate

Jesus was compassionate. Jesus demonstrated His love and compassion as He moved from village to village teaching, healing, driving out demons, and feeding the hungry. The Four Gospels are filled with stories that teach us that we must have compassion for others if we are to be like Jesus.

Take the lepers. Few people in Jesus' day wanted to be near them. We can't blame them. Leprosy was thought to be contagious, and not many were willing to take such a risk. Besides, most people in that day looked on illness, especially leprosy, as punishment for sin. Lepers were isolated and put out of the village. I suppose leprosy was a little like AIDS is today. We are fearful of those who have the AIDS virus, and we tend to think that most who get AIDS have no one to blame but themselves.

When Jesus first began His ministry, a man with leprosy came to Him and begged to be healed. Mark tells us what Jesus did: "Filled with compassion, Jesus reached out his hand and touched the man. 'I am willing,' he said. 'Be clean!' Immediately the leprosy left him and he was cured" (Mark 1:41–42). It's remarkable that Jesus touched the man. No one touched a leper. No one but Jesus. "Filled with compassion, . . ." His great love.

In the second year of Jesus' ministry, the Pharisees and teachers of the law brought a woman caught in adultery and threw her down in front of Him. They knew that stoning was the penalty for this sin. So did Jesus. But the Pharisees hoped to trap Jesus with a question: "'Teacher,'" they said, "this woman was caught in the act of adultery. In the Law Moses commanded us to stone such women. Now what do you say?'" (John 8:4–5).

The woman was guilty. She knew it. I doubt if she had any hope of avoiding that stoning. I picture her on the ground, surrounded by her accusers—big, strong men, standing, looking down at her. She had no chance of escape, but from the corner of her eye she saw a finger writing on the ground. Jesus knelt beside her and she sensed His presence. No one knows for sure what He wrote. Several minutes passed as the Pharisees kept asking questions. Jesus didn't answer. Then, slowly He rose to His feet and faced them. "'If any one of you is without sin,'" He said, "'let him be the first to throw a stone at her'" (John 8:7). Silence. No one moved.

Once again Jesus stooped down beside the woman and wrote on the ground. I believe the message was for her alone. Jesus knew her pain, and He wanted to help her. Slowly the Pharisees and religious leaders moved away— one by one. No one was left but Jesus and the woman. He didn't condemn her. "'Go now and leave your life of sin,'" He said. Jesus did not condone the woman's sin, but He had deep compassion for her. That's our goal: to be compassionate like Jesus.

Angry at Sin

Jesus was angry with sin. On several occasions Jesus became angry with the Pharisees. Once on the Sabbath a man with a withered hand was in the synagogue, and the

Pharisees watched to see if Jesus would heal him. Jesus knew their thoughts and asked, "'Is it lawful on the Sabbath to do good or to do evil, to save life or to kill?'" Then He "looked around at them with anger, being grieved by the hardness of their hearts" (Mark 3:5, NKJV).

A few days before Jesus was to die on the cross, He entered the temple court and found men selling animals for sacrifice—cattle, sheep, and doves. Sitting around at tables were money changers, men who hoped to make a profit from those who came to worship. This was the temple, a sacred place to worship God, to hear the reading of the Law, and to pray. Jesus took a whip and drove both the animals and the men from the temple area. "Get out of here!" He shouted. "How dare you turn My Father's house into a market!" That's anger. But the anger was directed at sin.

Jesus wept over Jerusalem. And on the cross He prayed for the Pharisees, the Sadducees, the Roman soldiers, the evildoers of the whole world: "'Father, forgive them; for they know not what they do'" (Luke 23:34, KJV).

If we want to be like Jesus, we must stand firm against the evil of burning and destroying places of worship today. We should be angry when children and the elderly are abused, when we find pornography in the marketplace, or when we discover dishonesty in our government. Our anger should burn when we see unknowing people being led into astrology and witchcraft or when murder and theft and destruction of property takes place all around us. These are sinful practices and deserve our anger. Paul wrote, "In your anger do not sin" (Eph. 4:26). He was right. Jesus had deep compassion and love for the people whom evil was destroying; He acted to correct the evil. That's constructive anger. And it's costly.

Aristotle expressed it well when he said, "Anybody can become angry—that is easy; but to be angry with the right person, and to the right degree, and at the right time, and for the right purpose, and in the right way—that is not easy."

No, it isn't easy. Too often I find myself getting angry about some evil I'm not even willing to fight. When this happens, I have to ask if I really love the people evil is destroying as Jesus loves them. Is my anger constructive enough to send me to work in the local drug abuse or crisis center? To write a letter to my congressman? To counsel with someone caught in evil's snare?

Just recently, two teenagers slashed the ragtop of a new convertible that a man in our town had just purchased. That would have caused any one of us to become angry! It's true, the owner was angry indeed; but when he was brought face to face with the young men, he asked to talk with them alone. He discovered their deep hurts and frustrations, and he realized they didn't know Jesus. When the boys agreed to work for him until they earned enough to pay for a new ragtop, the man began a friendship that in time would turn the boys' lives around. That is constructive anger.

Two major questions: Are we really angry with sin? And are we willing to actively, constructively fight against it? We have to answer those questions if we want to be like Jesus.

Willing to Pray

Jesus spent time in prayer. If Jesus, the Son of God, felt the need to spend time with the Father in prayer, how much greater is our need? Jesus prayed at His baptism, and the Father sent the Holy Spirit upon Him. He spent the night in prayer before choosing the twelve disciples. Throughout His ministry He often withdrew from the crowds and from His disciples to pray. The disciples took notice. "Teach us to pray," they said to Jesus, so He did.

At one time I wondered why God gave John the seventeenth chapter of his Gospel to share with us. It's a prayer of Jesus, intimate and from the heart. Why would God share this special time—Father and Son in close, caring relationship? I believe the purpose is to show us the relationship Abba, Father desires with us. From His heart, Jesus poured out His deepest concerns to the Father. He prayed for those closest to Him—His disciples. Then He prayed for those who would come to know Him, for believers of all generations to come—for you and for me. "That all of them may be one, Father, just as You are in Me and I am in You." That's what He asked.

Jesus knew the Father's plan. He knew His purpose in coming to earth: to bring believers into His kingdom, to give eternal life to all those who would answer His call. "I want those You have given Me to be with Me where I am," Jesus told the Father.

Have there been times that you enjoyed this close, intimate time with Abba, Father? Jesus liked to find a quiet place, often "up the mountain." But today many of us are surrounded by noise, people, and distractions of every kind. Susanna Wesley, mother of fifteen children including John and Charles, often threw her apron over her head to pray. When the children saw the apron go up, they knew mother was praying. God hears us no matter where we are, and He'll welcome us into His presence. He loves us. If we want to be like Jesus, we must spend time with Him in prayer.

Called to Be a Reflection of Jesus

A reflection of Jesus—that's His plan for us. We might think this an impossible goal if we did not have the disciples' lives before us. Look at Peter. When Jesus first called him, he was a rough and rowdy fisherman. He thought he knew it all. He made quick decisions. He was determined to change God's plan, but deep in his heart Peter wanted to please Jesus. He wanted to follow Him. It just took awhile for him to change. Peter became the chief spokesman to the Jewish authorities. He was the leader of the Jewish church and the first missionary to the Gentiles. He suffered because, like Jesus, he could not stop telling others about God's plan once he understood it. He wanted everyone he knew to be in God's family. Peter was a reflection of Jesus.

So were the other disciples—all but Judas, who chose to follow a different master. Yes, in time Jesus' disciples were focused on His plan. Patient, compassionate, angry with sin, and men of prayer. They were like Jesus.

But what about today? Do you know believers who are reflections of Jesus? I do. I see His love and patience in my friend Fran as she cares for her ninety-four-year-old mother. I see His compassion in my friends Wilma and Luella as they prepare meals for the sick and in the faces of those in my care group who help a young minister meet the needs of the homeless in Los Angeles. I've seen His anger against evil in Kathleen, a lovely lady in San Diego who comforts the families of homosexuals and AIDS patients. I have seen His joy in a counselor I know when he was instrumental in reconciling a couple who had a hard time forgiving each other. Perhaps greatest of all, I've seen Jesus' peace reflected in so many when they've been with Jesus in prayer. They are people called to be reflections of Jesus, focused on His plan.

Are you overwhelmed? Discouraged? Think the goal is impossible to reach? God knew this would happen, and He provided a way. He sent His Spirit.

Discovering His Plan

1. Romans 8:28–29 tells us that those who love God are "to be conformed to the likeness of his Son." Peter wrote that we are to "follow in his steps" (1 Pet. 2:21). Just what do these words mean to you personally?

2. In one sentence, state the primary goal of your life. How do you plan to accomplish your goal?

3. What characteristics do you see in Jesus Christ which you feel need further development in your life? What are some things you can do to become more like Jesus?

4. On the positive side, name three ways you were a reflection of Jesus this past week.

7

Empowered by His Spirit

So we're in God's family. We're His children, and we know we are to serve. But how can we become more like Jesus? How can we find our ministry? And how can we obey God's call on our lives? We can't unless we are empowered by His Spirit.

I don't know about you, but it took me awhile to learn about the Holy Spirit. I knew about Jesus from the time I learned to sing "Jesus Loves Me." I knew about the Father when I was taught to pray, "Our Father, who art in heaven." The Holy Spirit? I've been a slow learner, but I've learned. Now the joy of living day by day in the power of the Holy Spirit makes me eager to share with you some of the things I have learned, things I know to be true.

The Holy Spirit Is God

Like the Father and the Son, the Holy Spirit was present and at work in the creation, "hovering over the waters" (Gen. 1:2). John Calvin suggests that this act of the Spirit was either to sustain the creation or to cherish it. Sustain and cherish. From Genesis to Revelation we find the Spirit working with the Father and the Son. It is by the Spirit's gentle persuasion that we are drawn into the family of God when we believe. It is the Spirit who lovingly empowers us to live within God's plan and do the work of ministry. Our God is a Triune God, one God in three persons: Father, Son, and Holy Spirit, equal in power and honor.

Have you noticed that many titles are used for the Spirit in our Bible? Among others, He is called the Spirit of God, Spirit of the Lord God, Spirit of the Father, Spirit of the Son, and Spirit of Christ. Some titles speak of His work: the Spirit of Grace, of Holiness, of Life, of Adoption, and of Glory. John speaks of the Helper and the Eternal Spirit. Found only three times in the Old Testament, the title Holy Spirit is used ninety-one times in the New Testament—more than any other title. Each title adds to our understanding of the third Person of the Trinity.

Paul tells us that no one knows the thoughts of God except the Spirit of God (1 Cor. 2:11). The Spirit, then, is all knowing. He has all wisdom, and He is present everywhere. I like the words of David in Psalm 139:7–10:

> Where can I go from your Spirit?
>> Where can I flee from your presence?
> If I go up to the heavens, you are there;
>> if I make my bed in the depths, you are there.
> If I rise on the wings of the dawn,
>> if I settle on the far side of the sea,
> even there your hand will guide me,
>> your right hand will hold me fast.

Most importantly, we know that the Holy Spirit is indeed God and deserves our respect and honor and worship. Peter reminded Ananias of this truth when he asked,

"'Ananias, how is it that Satan has so filled your heart that you have lied to the Holy Spirit and have kept for yourself some of the money you received for the land? . . . You have not lied to men but to God'" (Acts 5:3–4).

The Revealing of the Spirit

Do you think of God as having a personality? I do, because we are made in His image. Jesus revealed the personality of God when He came and lived among us, teaching us of His loving, caring nature. Like the Father and the Son, the Holy Spirit has personality. He loves us, comforts us, helps us, and is grieved when we fail to follow His leading; but we cannot see the Spirit. We can only come to know Him through our innermost being, our spirits.

If you like good literature, as I do, then you know that writers often use symbols to bridge the material and invisible worlds. Our understanding is enhanced by bringing together some truth, some spiritual reality, with something we can see and touch. This is called symbolism. Our flag is a symbol of our country and carries a deeper meaning than the cloth material. The cross that we wear on a chain comes together in our minds with Jesus' sacrifice, redemption, and salvation. Jesus used a lamp, bread, seed, a farmer, and a shepherd, along with many other concrete objects, to teach invisible truths. Throughout the Bible, our understanding of spiritual truths is enriched by the many words that carry symbolic as well as literal meanings. God has used a number of symbols to help us understand the Holy Spirit. Let's look at three.

A Dove

Above the altar in our church is a beautiful dove carved out of rosewood by one of our members. It is about six feet in diameter, and if you look closely you will see that the wings are shaped to form the word *Jesus*. It is a constant reminder of the close relationship of Jesus and the

Holy Spirit. The symbol of the dove representing the invisible Spirit also speaks of gentleness, one of the traits associated with this little bird. It speaks of faithfulness because we are told that doves have only one mate. It speaks of innocence. Jesus said, "'Be as shrewd as snakes and as innocent as doves'" (Matt. 10:16). It speaks of life and peace because Noah sent out the dove who brought back an olive leaf as proof that the forty days of rain were over. Last, the white dove, used in Bible days as a sacrifice by those who could not afford a lamb, speaks of the sacrifice of the innocent Son of God. Gentle, faithful, innocent, life giving, peaceful, and truthful teacher: the Holy Spirit.

Streams of Living Water

At the Feast of Tabernacles in Jerusalem, Jesus spoke to a crowd of Jews who were debating whether or not He was the Christ. Many in the crowd put their faith in Him, but others refused to believe. Then Jesus called in a loud voice, "'If anyone is thirsty, let him come to me and drink. Whoever believes in me, as the Scripture has said, streams of living water will flow from within him.'" The apostle John adds, "By this he meant the Spirit, whom those who believed in him were later to receive" (John 7:37–38). This symbol is especially significant because nothing can live without water—not plants, not animals, not people. Neither do we live in Christ Jesus unless we have His Spirit within us.

When Jesus met the Samaritan woman by the well, He said to her, "'If you knew the gift of God and who it is that asks you for a drink, you would have asked him and he would have given you living water'" (John 4:10). Later, in a vision of the new Jerusalem which John received, Jesus said, "'To him who is thirsty I will give to drink without cost from the spring of the water of life'" (Rev. 21:6). God's Spirit flows through believers like a stream, filling, refreshing, and giving new life; but this water does not flow in those outside God's family. Peter, in warning about false teachers said they were "springs without water" (2 Pet. 2:17). Without water, there is no life.

A Seal

In ancient times, kings wore a ring that bore their seal. When the ring was pressed into wax placed on an object, the king's seal was imprinted. This was a mark of ownership. King Xerxes, for example, commanded Mordecai to seal his decree concerning the Jews with his signet ring, "'for no document written in the king's name and sealed with his ring can be revoked'" (Esther 8:8). When Daniel was thrown into the lions' den, the king sealed the stone placed over the opening with his ring (Dan. 7:17). The stone could only be removed by the king's orders. The seal was a sign of ownership and authority.

In the first century, the Romans used seals to close important documents or packages. Today messages carried by military attachés bear government seals denoting ownership. Only the person authorized can break the seal.

Paul understood that the seal was a symbol of the Holy Spirit when he wrote to the believers at Ephesus: "And you also were included in Christ when you heard the word of truth, the gospel of your salvation. Having believed, you were marked in him with a seal, the promised Holy Spirit; who is a deposit guaranteeing our inheritance until the redemption of those who are God's possession—to the praise of his glory" (Eph. 1:13–14).

"In Christ." Born into His family. The moment we believed we were marked as His, sealed with His Holy Spirit. A gentle dove, a stream of living water, and a seal of ownership—these symbols help us to understand the Holy Spirit, the third Person of the Trinity, "Christ in you, the hope of glory." No wonder Paul wrote, "Praise be to the God and Father of our Lord Jesus Christ who has blessed us in the heavenly realms with every spiritual blessing in Christ" (Eph. 1:3).

The Work of the Spirit

Suppose we had lived during the time Jesus walked the earth, teaching, healing, and calling people to follow Him. How would we have reacted when He was crucified and rose from the dead? Would we have believed the reports of the apostles that Jesus had risen and had appeared to them? Would we have been among the 120 who gathered in the upper room to pray and wait?

I've often wondered why so few gathered there when thousands had heard Him speak and been told about God's plan for building His kingdom, but a remnant believed. They knew what Jesus had told the apostles, and they waited expectantly for His words to be fulfilled: "'Do not leave Jerusalem, but wait for the gift my Father promised, which you have heard me speak about. For John baptized with water, but in a few days you will be baptized with the Holy Spirit. . . . You will receive power when the Holy Spirit comes on you; and you will be My witnesses in Jerusalem, and in all Judea and Samaria, and to the ends of the earth'" (Acts 1:4–5, 8, NKJV).

Surely, too, the believers gathered in that upper room remembered the promise of God delivered by the prophet Joel: "'I will pour out my Spirit on all people. Your sons and daughters will prophesy, your old men will dream dreams, your young men will see visions. Even on my servants, both men and women, I will pour out my Spirit in those days'" (Joel 2:28–29).

Most likely all those gathered that day in Jerusalem had been baptized with water. They understood John's baptism of repentance, but baptism with the Holy Spirit was not so easily understood. They knew that God's Spirit came upon prophets, priests, judges, and kings that they might be empowered to speak for God and do His work among men. But was the Spirit to be given to simple fishermen and shopkeepers? To men and women who held no special leadership positions in the Jewish community? Was the outpouring of the Spirit for all believers?

Indeed it was. On the day of Pentecost, "a sound like the blowing of a violent wind came from heaven and filled the whole house where they were sitting. They saw what seemed to be tongues of fire that separated and came to rest on each of them. All of them were filled with the Holy Spirit and began to speak in other tongues as the Spirit enabled them" (Acts 2:4).

That promise is for us too. When we come to that moment of belief, we are born anew, baptized into the family of God and filled with His Spirit. This gift of the Spirit is God's seal upon us. God's Word tells us that "If anyone does not have the Spirit of Christ, he does not belong to Christ" (Rom. 8:9). God knew that we could never live lives pleasing to Him without help. The work of the Holy Spirit is to empower us as believers to live our lives within God's plan and to do the work of ministry.

Empowerment to Live within God's Plan

First, the Spirit remolds our character. Testimonies of the Spirit's work in changing the lives of those who have been on drugs or in prison or in some cult are often more memorable than the testimonies of those brought up in strong Christian homes. But we all come into His family in the same way—sinners saved through faith in Jesus Christ. As a potter molds unruly clay into a beautiful vessel, so the Holy Spirit begins His work of molding us into the image of God. Oswald Sanders' poem, "In the Hand of the Potter" says it all:

> To the Potter's house I went down one day,
> And watched him while molding a vessel of clay,
> And many a wonderful lesson I drew
> As I noted the process the clay passed through.

Trampled and broken, downtrodden and rolled,
To render it plastic and fit for the mould.
How like the clay that is human, I thought,
Which in heavenly hands to God's image is brought,
For self must be cast as the dust at His feet
Ere man is renewed, and for service made meet;
And pride must be broken, and self-will lost—
All laid on the altar, whatever the cost;
And all that is boasted of human display
Must yield to God's hand and be taken away.[1]

I remember Keith, a young student who came to me one day and asked, "Is it prideful when you know you are becoming more loving, joyful, peaceful, and patient—you know, when you can see all the fruits of the Spirit found in Galatians 5 becoming a part of your character?" I, too, could see the changes in Keith and assured him that God must be pleased that he was allowing the Spirit to work in his life. Today, Keith is a strong role model for those in the church he pastors in Three Rivers, California.

When we ask, the Spirit is our willing Helper in overcoming harmful habits. Jan, a beautiful Christian who is daily growing in Christ, recently told me how the Spirit empowered her to quit smoking. "I had attempted to stop this habit many times," Jan said, "I knew it was hurting my body, but nothing worked. As my faith in Christ grew, so did my belief that He was the only One who could solve my problem. I began to pray in earnest that He would help me. On July 31, 1991, at 3:00 A.M. I awakened from sleep, got out of bed, walked to the kitchen, and emptied a full package of cigarettes onto the counter. I took a pair of scissors out of a drawer and cut each cigarette into little pieces. I know the Holy Spirit was with me because I have not smoked a cigarette since."

Second, the Spirit leads us into prayer. As the Holy Spirit remolds our character and strengthens us to give up harmful habits, He gives us the desire to spend more time in prayer—to praise God, thank Him, listen to Him, and seek His help. At times we do not know what to pray, and the Spirit brings needs to our mind. God has chosen to work through His people to meet the needs of others. The Holy Spirit may awaken us from sleep to pray for some member of our family, a friend, a neighbor, or someone who needs His touch at the moment. He may nudge us to pray for the homeless man sitting on the sidewalk as we enter the supermarket, for the mother struggling with her unruly child, for the teenagers shouting obscenities at passersby. If we do not pray for others as the Holy Spirit places their needs before us, who will?

Third, the Spirit leads us into the Word. Not only does the Holy Spirit encourage us to be more open to pray, but He gives us a hunger for the Word of God. In my own life, this was a turning point. Although our family was always in church on Sundays and I thought of myself as a good Christian, my Bible gathered dust during the week. I was teaching at the local college and spent hours reading both English and American literature, but I read my Bible only on Sundays—in church following the pastor's sermon reference. Other than the work of the Holy Spirit, I have no explanation for the hunger which I suddenly had for God's Word. I found myself racing home from the campus and devouring the Four Gospels. When I went to my pastor with questions, he suggested that I slow down and let the Spirit teach me verse by verse. That was good advice. For four months I read, studied, and prayed as the Spirit opened the Word to my understanding. Then in the spring, I proposed a course in Bible literature to my department head. It was approved and placed in the fall catalogue. What a blessing it was for me to teach the Bible to hundreds of eager students for the next twelve years!

If you do not have a hunger for God's Word, pray that the Spirit will give you this deep desire. He speaks to us through His Word, teaching us, counseling us, or correct-ing us. He often uses the Word to lead us into ministry.

Empowerment for the Work of Ministry

Truth: Every Christian has a ministry assignment. Chris-tians usually think about ministry in terms of serving the Lord as the pastor of a church, as an evangelist who trav-els, or as a missionary who is called to serve God in a for-eign country. If we're generous with our definition, we include those serving on full-time staff of organizations like Campus Crusade, InterVarsity, or the Navigators. But as Christians, we are in full-time service to our Lord, and our mission fields are wherever He has placed us at the moment—school, home, church, work, or foreign field. I like this definition of a minister: "A servant appointed to transact or manage business under the authority of another, one who does good, who is helpful, who provides for the needs of others." The definition is straight out of the dictionary and right on target for the Christian.

Let me illustrate. Several years ago two high-ranking air force officers were in a meeting to determine the next assignment for a bright, young air force captain. Both men wanted Captain Richard Engel, but one assignment would lead to a brilliant career, the other to a dead end. As they debated their decision, the captain waited in the outer office reading a magazine. It was evident that he was enjoying the break from the day's busy schedule. Occa-sionally a relaxed smile crossed his face as he turned a page. When he rose and casually poured himself a cup of coffee, the secretary asked, "How can you be so relaxed? Don't you realize your career is at stake? The decision being made by the generals can make or break you!"

Captain Engel chuckled. "I'm not concerned," he said. "I work hard and do the best job I can. My superiors' opinion of my work matters to me, but I'm on the staff of the King, and He has veto power!"

On the staff of the King doing the King's business. That sounds like an important assignment. And it is. It is God's plan that every believer have a ministry. Our ministries are a part of His master plan.

Truth: Every Christian has spiritual gifts. When we come into God's family, the Holy Spirit gives us special gifts to enable us to accomplish the work He assigns us, but we cannot separate these spiritual gifts from the church established by our Lord Jesus Christ. The church is the family of God, the body of Christ, called to live and work within His plan. The gifts of the Spirit are not the fruits of the Spirit which He seeks to mold into our characters, and they are not the natural talents or abilities which we all have, although the Spirit may choose to gift us in these areas. Rather, the spiritual gifts are the unique function of the Holy Spirit working through us within the body of Christ to build up the body and make it more Christlike.

While the Spirit empowers us, He does not take away our free will. We have the ability to use our gifts under His direction to the fullest extent in God's service. Or, we can misuse or ignore the gifts. Peter's advice was that "each one should use whatever gift he has received to serve others, faithfully administering God's grace in its various forms" (1 Pet. 4:10).

While various spiritual gifts are mentioned throughout God's Word, we can make a list of those mentioned in Romans 12, 1 Corinthians 12, and Ephesians 4. Let's briefly consider these.

Prophesy. In the New Testament we read of prophets in Jerusalem, Antioch, and Corinth (Acts 11:27; 13:1; 1 Cor. 12:28). Agabus, Judas, and Silas are named as men who had this gift of prophesy (Acts 21:10; 15:32). Today, as in this earlier time, the Spirit clarifies the plans of God for His people through His Word. Those who have the gift of pastor, teacher, and evangelist, also have this gift.

Serving. Stephen, who was later stoned to death, and Philip, who ministered to the Ethiopian, were two men in the early church who had this gift of serving (Acts 6:5). Today many use this gift of helping others by cooking and cleaning for those who are ill, repairing broken items in homes and churches, explaining business matters to widows, meeting whatever day-to-day needs the Spirit reveals.

Pastor / Teacher. John surely had this gift as his compassion for his flock comes through his words, "My dear children." He was concerned about their welfare and eager to teach them spiritual truths. We expect to find this gift in the pastor of our church and in those who teach Sunday school and care groups. The person with this gift has a deep concern for those in his care and eagerly feeds his flock from God's Word.

Encourager. Paul, Barnabas, and Silas were great encouragers (Acts 11:22–23; 16:40; 20:1). We all know people with the gift to lift us up when we are down, people who can challenge us to move forward. An encourager is one who can often redirect our thinking from negative to positive and map out a course of action for us.

Giving. The Spirit gives some people the ability not only to build resources and to make money, but also the ability to discern the needs of God's people and His church. The person who has this gift joyfully and eagerly gives of his resources to meet the material needs of God's people and to advance the work of God's plan, without any thought of gain for himself.

Leadership. This gift is sometimes called the gift of administration. This is the ability to set goals that will advance God's plan and lead others to work toward those goals (Acts 15:7–11; 1 Tim. 5:17). This gift is often seen in members of church boards or elders, in those who oversee the work of the church office, and in heads of various ministries.

Mercy. At various times in our lives we all must comfort those who are sick or suffering from the loss of a loved one. The person with the gift of mercy has a deep compassion for those with physical, mental, or emotional problems and can meet their needs effectively. Those with this gift are found visiting in hospitals and nursing homes and helping the pastor comfort the bereaved.

Evangelist. Peter and Paul quickly come to our minds when we think of New Testament people who had this gift. Billy Graham is our primary example of an evangelist today, but this spiritual gift is enjoyed by many who have a deep desire to share the gospel with unbelievers and lead them to become Jesus' disciples.

Apostles. Most people today believe that this gift was given to the eleven men who were personally taught by Jesus and served Him until their death, and to Paul whom Jesus called on the road to Damascus. Paul listed the marks of an apostle as "signs, wonders, and miracles" (Gal. 2:8). This gift enabled these men to lead many churches and to assume authority in spiritual matters.

Wisdom. Peter said that Paul wrote "with the wisdom that God gave him" (2 Pet. 3:15). Paul explains this gift of wisdom by distinguishing between the wisdom of man and God's secret wisdom which is revealed by His Spirit (1 Cor. 2:13). This gift is the ability to speak spiritual truth when an issue requires a difficult choice.

Knowledge. Paul wrote that in Christ "are hidden all the treasures of wisdom and knowledge" (Col. 2:3). Those with the gift of knowledge have the unique ability to understand God's Word and His plan, to gather and clarify information. They are able to help others to understand these truths from Christ Jesus.

Faith. Hebrews 11 is a roll call of men of faith. "Faith is being sure of what we hope for and certain of what we do not see" (v. 1). It is the ability to believe God's promises with an absolute certainty. Those with this gift can then move the body of believers into claiming the promises of God, relying on Him to do great things in His church.

Healing. Peter surely had this gift, and people brought their sick to him to be healed (Acts 3:1–10; 5:15–16; 9:32–35). This gift enables a person to serve as an intermediary through whom God works to heal others of physical or emotional illnesses. Most often those who have the gift of healing are strong people of prayer.

Miracles. God did miracles through both Peter and Paul (Acts 9:36–42; 19:11–12). While we tend to discount many of the extraordinary things that happen today as miracles, God is no less powerful. He does work through many people to perform acts that are indeed miracles.

Discerning of Spirits. John spoke of testing the spirits "to see whether they are from God" (1 John 4:1–6). Those with this gift have the ability to determine whether certain behavior or teaching is from God or from Satan. They can sense the difference and thus prevent false teaching and confusion from infiltrating the church.

Languages/Tongues. When the King James Bible was translated in 1611, the word *tongues* meant what we think of today as "languages." Three instances in the Book of Acts indicate this gift was used and understood by those who heard: at Pentecost (Acts 2), in Caesarea (Acts 10), and in Ephesus (Acts 19). The gift is the ability to speak a language without previous study or knowledge. Many believe this gift is active today in missionaries who must quickly learn to speak with those of another culture.

In 1 Corinthians 14, Paul referred to some who have the ability to speak a language not understood either by themselves or by their hearers. Today this is known as *glossolalia* or a heavenly language. As a language directed to God, many feel that it enriches their devotional life. Others see no spiritual reality in it. We should not try to impose our own way or judgment on others regardless of which way we interpret Paul's teaching about this practice.

Interpretation of a Language/Tongue. As a companion gift to languages/tongues, this gift enables a person to understand and interpret a language that he hears but has not previously learned. Paul wrote: "Anyone who speaks in a tongue should pray that he may interpret what he says. . . . In the church I would rather speak five intelligible words to instruct others than ten thousand words in a tongue" (1 Cor. 14:13, 19).

We need to take to heart the truth of Corinthians 13 as it applies to all the spiritual gifts. There Paul affirmed that the greatest gift of all is love. Without love, we will fail in using any one of the gifts.

Truth: We need to know our spiritual gifts. Most often the Spirit reveals our gifts to us by helping us realize that we are unusually successful in a particular ministry. Other believers recognize our ability to serve, to evangelize, to teach, or to perform some other task—and often comment on it. If you have not yet discovered your spiritual gifts, your pastor or someone else who has observed you in various ministries may help you. Or you may just need to step out and try new ministries where you feel led to serve and see if you are effective. Certainly the ministry God has chosen for you and the gifts He has given you will bring great inward joy and a sense of fulfillment.

Another way to discover your gifts is to explore some of the many books written by biblical scholars for this purpose. Spiritual gift profiles can often pinpoint your gifts if you will answer some questions. Be open to more than one gift. Our God is generous in blessing us!

Sometimes the Spirit gives us additional gifts that are needed in the body of Christ for particular ministries. In his book *Christian Excellence*, Jon Johnston tells how his mom discovered a spiritual gift. She was a quiet, shy woman and a committed Christian. Recognition of the gift of serving began when she entered a local baking contest and won first place. She entered another, and again she won. She became known as a great cook, and her ministry was started. The Holy Spirit had given her the spiritual gift of serving which she used by baking cookies, cakes, and pies for those in convalescent homes in her town. Within a short time people began calling to thank her and were sharing their problems. This opened up a way for her to use another gift—the gift of encouragement.[2]

God does not want us to be weak servants. He wants us to be secure, confident, and knowledgeable. When Jesus calls us to a ministry, His Spirit within us will empower us to do the work. Every believer has spiritual gifts, and we are all part of God's plan. We are His ministers. We are on His staff. First, however, we need to understand who we are in God's family, our position in His kingdom. Like the disciples, we may need a new vision.

Discovering His Plans

1. In one sentence each, answer the following: (a) Who is our God? (b) Who is the Holy Spirit?

2. In what way do symbols add to your understanding of the Holy Spirit? What symbol is most meaningful to you? Explain.

3. Give an example of a person whose life reflects evidence of the Holy Spirit's work. What specific evidence do you see?

4. What gives you assurance that the Holy Spirit is remolding your character?

5. Have you discovered your spiritual gifts? If so, how are you using these gifts? If not, what plans do you have for *discovering them*?

8

Called to a New Vision

My dad was a Texas rancher, and he worked hard keeping every acre beautiful. White-faced Hereford cattle grazed on pastures of green grass in the spring, and sweet-smelling hay filled the barns to the top, ready for the winter months. Tanks of fresh water were spaced across the pasture near clumps of trees that provided shade for the cows on warm days. A strong fence surrounded the entire ranch.

Still, Dad did not realize how much more he could do until one day a friend took him up for his first airplane ride. Dad was seventy-five at the time and fearless—that is, as long as his feet were planted firmly on God's green earth; but that September day Dad decided to let go of his fear of flying. He put his trust in Ed Littlejohn, the pilot of that little two-seater aircraft. As they flew over the ranch from border to border, Dad could see for miles. For the first time he got a clear, broad picture of the whole ranch. He came down with a renewed excitement, full of plans, new ideas, and things he wanted to do to make the ranch more productive. He had a new vision.

That's how it is when we let go of our fears and allow God to lift us high above our little worlds. He has called us to be a part of His larger plan, and He wants us to get a broader, clearer vision of who we are and what He expects of us, His children, members of His own family.

You may feel a little bit like my dad before he got his new vision—afraid to fly. Or you may identify with my young friend, Travis, who was excited about his new swimming class—until the day his coach decided his fledgling student had coasted long enough. You see, Travis was content to sit on the side of the pool, dangling his feet and watching the swimmers. On this particular day the coach said to him, "You can't be a spectator forever. Not in my class. Get into the water!"

Children of the King were not called to be spectators forever—that we know! But why do we sometimes act as if being a pew-sitter was our calling? Abraham Maslow, the psychologist, once stated that only one person in a hundred is fully alive. The other ninety-nine realize only about 10 percent of their potential. They see only 10 percent of the world's beauty, hear only 10 percent of the world's music and poetry, and draw back from God's desire for their lives to the point where they survive with only a shriveled capacity for giving and receiving love. Why? Do we have a limited vision of who we are in Christ Jesus? Do we need to expand our vision? Do we understand what it means to be in the service of the King? Good questions. Pursuing the answers could lead us to a new vision.

Know Who You Are

There is no such thing as a plain, ordinary believer. The word *Christian* means "little anointed one." Each of us is chosen to be a child of the King. Jesus said, "Ye have not chosen me, but I have chosen you" (John 15:16, KJV). Just like the twelve disciples! Paul wrote that Jesus, through His death on the cross, has brought us right into the very presence of God. We stand before Him with no charges against us—not one! (Col. 1:22).

How does God see us? We are special. Children of the King. Chosen. Greatly loved. Redeemed royalty. Members of His own family. Like the disciples.

Did Jesus teach the disciples that they were related to the King who would sit on David's throne? Indeed He did. Jesus came announcing that He was this promised King. He told the disciples that they were to rule over the twelve tribes of Israel. That was exciting news! James and John even asked to sit on His right hand and on His left when He came into His kingdom. Peter, James, and John had seen Jesus in all His heavenly glory at the transfiguration—and they liked what they saw. On their last trip into Jerusalem with Jesus, the disciples fought all the way over who was to be the greatest in the kingdom of God.

I suppose every one of them wanted to be prime minister, but their vision was too small. Like Dad, their feet were firmly planted on the ground. They were wrapped up in their own little worlds, thinking of an immediate, earthly kingdom rather than the larger spiritual one Jesus had in mind. They didn't understand the plans of God's heart.

Many Christians today have the same problem the disciples had: limited vision. Psychologists sometimes use a simple test to measure how people view life in this world. The person taking the test is shown a blank piece of paper with a small black dot in the center. "What do you see?" the psychologist asks. Most people respond, "I see a black dot." They miss the big sheet of paper.

If we fail to understand the work the King of kings has planned for us as members of His family, we too have limited vision. We're missing the big picture. Jesus chose a special time to enlarge the vision of His disciples. The lesson is for us as well.

Expand Your Vision

Jesus' earthly ministry was drawing to a close. Five days before Passover, the crowds welcomed Him into Jerusalem with shouts of "Hosanna!" "Blessed is he who comes in the name of the Lord!" "Blessed is the King of Israel!" (John 12:13). King of Israel! Those were the words the disciples heard. A few days later when they met in the upper room to observe the Passover feast, they were filled with anticipation of Jesus bringing in His kingdom. Imagine their smiles as they went through the ritual of the Passover feast. They must have felt grand seated at the table with the future King of Israel. They had completely forgotten that only a short time before Jesus had been teaching them that He must suffer, be rejected, be killed, and after three days rise again (Mark 8:31).

At the end of the feast, it was customary for the master of the feast to pronounce a benediction. Jesus did something entirely different. As He arose from the table He knew the thoughts of His disciples. Somehow, He must change their vision—enlarge it and help them to understand His broader plan. He could have worn a robe bordered with the ribbon of an honored and distinguished rabbi. Instead, He took up a towel, the sign of a servant. Then He poured water into a basin and began to wash His disciples' feet. This was not difficult for Jesus to do because He knew who He was. He knew His mission. He had absolute trust and confidence in His Father's plan, but the whole idea of Jesus doing the work of a servant was revolting to Peter. Washing feet—anyone's feet—was beneath the majesty, the dignity, and the honor that belonged to his King. Peter's vision of his own mission was certainly not that of a lowly servant.

Has someone you love and admire ever washed your feet? I once went to a retreat held at one of the missions in northern California. On Saturday night we gathered in a large room for a Communion service. But before serving Communion, the leaders of the retreat announced that they wanted to wash our feet. During that week we had drawn close to our leaders and had become aware of their deep love of Jesus. It shone in their faces and was reflected in their actions. We knew they loved us and had in many ways sacrificed to come and teach us, but nothing touched us quite as much as the moment they knelt before us and tenderly washed our feet. I don't know about the others, but I felt unworthy. I wanted to reverse our positions. The tears would not stop. That night I experienced a little of what Peter must have felt seeing Jesus on His knees serving him.

Changing the vision of becoming a prime minister to becoming a lowly servant is not an easy task. It was not easy for Peter or for the disciples, and it is not easy for us. Some of us struggle with wanting to be served rather than wanting to serve. Others of us struggle with feeling insecure as Christians, embarrassed to admit we have much to learn, even though we are zealous in good works. Both these problems can lead to working hard for the wrong reasons and the wrong goal.

Indeed, Jesus had some radical ideas of what it means to be a child of the King. His ideas take awhile to grasp—and to put into practice. He taught Peter, and He teaches us, that we cannot be the greatest; we must be the least. We cannot be the King; we must serve the King. We cannot be prime ministers; we must be servants.

Understand What It Means to Be a Servant of the King

As believers some of us may be called to ministries that will thrust us into worldwide recognition. This was true for Billy Graham, for Louis Palau, and for Alexander Solzhenitsyn. On the other hand, God may give us the ministry of visiting the sick, gathering food for the hungry, or caring for the little children in the church nursery—and only a few people will ever know what we do. All our work for God is important. We serve where He has placed us: in our homes, in our churches, in our communities, or in our nation. Every place we go, in everything we do, we are part of His plan. He sends us forth as His servants. The world will come to know Jesus through our loving service in all walks of life.

A Servant Serves

We all know Christians who long ago learned what it means to take up the work of a child of the King, to be His servant. We immediately think of Mother Teresa who has served the poor in India since 1929. Or we remember some beloved pastor who is always there to comfort the sick, the dying, and the heartbroken. We wonder why we still struggle with pride, desire for recognition, and honor. It's encouraging to observe the slow-changing attitude of the disciples. By the time they became well-known apostles, leaders in the early church, and honored men, their vision was in line with God's plan. They learned to serve.

Many of us are still in the learning process. Not too long after my experience at the retreat when I thought I had learned a valuable lesson about servanthood, I was asked to teach at an InterVarsity Christian Fellowship camp near Watsonville, California. Armed with Bible, notes, and a head full of ideas, I met my students the first evening around the dinner table. They were a lively group from a number of colleges in the area, eager to learn, and full of questions. At the close of the meal, I noticed that the staff man at the head of the table next to mine rose and started clearing the table. *What's wrong with those students?* I thought. *Why are they letting their teacher clear the table?*

My resentment grew as the IV staffer, having completed his task, came to my table and began to remove the dishes. "What's going on?" I whispered to him. "I certainly can't sit here and let you clear my table!" When he just smiled and said, "It's OK," I rose and silently helped him.

Following breakfast the next morning, the pattern was repeated. But this time, several of the students offered to help. By the evening meal, students all over the dining hall were doing what they had watched their teachers do. I had been taught another lesson in servanthood—a lesson Jesus so lovingly taught His disciples by example.

In an article titled "The Making of a Minister," Walter Wangerin Jr. tells how God used a man named Arthur to teach him to be a servant. When Arthur became housebound, no one in the church wanted to visit him. Why should they? Arthur had a "burping contempt for his fellow parishioners." But week after week the pastor spent time with Arthur in his filthy room, filled with roaches, moldy newspapers, and cigarette smoke.

When Arthur was no longer able to care for himself, he asked his pastor to dress him. In those times, the pastor learned to love Arthur Ford. He began to understand the words *ministry*, *service*, and *discipleship*. "In the terrible, terrible DOING of ministry," Walter Wangerin writes, "the minister is born.[1]

Jesus said that someday the King will say to us, "'I tell you the truth, whatever you did for one of the least of these brothers of mine, you did for me'" (Matt. 25:40). As Christians, our spiritual gifts may differ—but we are all servants. Sometimes we will be tired, weary, or discouraged. We may feel unappreciated. We may not like to change our plans so that we can take care of some task the Lord has assigned us, but we are to follow in the steps of Jesus. The King of kings was a servant.

A Servant Obeys

Of one thing we can be sure: when Jesus calls us to a new vision, He expects obedience. "'If you love me,'" He said, "'you will obey what I command'" (John 14:15). But as servants of Jesus Christ, we may experience moments of terrible conflict. We want His plan, but we also want our own plan. We pray, "Thy will be done," but we mean, "Let my will be done." We know Jesus expects us to obey, but we struggle to find a way out.

It helps to have Jesus' example of obedience to the Father before us. "'My food,'" Jesus said, "'is to do the will of him who sent me and to finish his work'" (John 4:34). That is our task as well: to do His will and to fulfill the mission He has given us—even when we don't feel qualified. Or we don't want to give up the necessary time. Or we can't see the end result.

The examples of some biblical characters who struggled with obedience encourage me when I'm tempted to draw back from something I know the Lord wants me to do. Take Moses, for example. His conversation with the Lord went like this when he was called to lead the Israelites:

Moses said to God, "Who am I, that I should go to Pharaoh and bring the Israelites out of Egypt?"

And God said, "I will be with you." . . .

"What if they do not believe me or listen to me and say 'The Lord did not appear to you?'" . . .

"If they do not believe you or pay attention to the first miraculous sign, they may believe the second." . . .

"O Lord, I have never been eloquent, neither in the past nor since you have spoken to your servant. I am slow of speech and tongue." . . .

"Now go; I will help you speak and will teach you what to say."

But Moses said, "O LORD, please send someone else to do it." (Exod. 3:11–12; 4:1, 8, 10, 12–13)

And remember Gideon? He didn't have much to qualify him for the job God called him to do, not in my way of thinking. In fact, Gideon was surprised that God even considered him. Listen to the conversation which took place between the angel of the Lord and Gideon:

"The LORD is with you, mighty warrior."

"But sir," Gideon replied, "if the LORD is with us, why has all this happened to us?". . .

The LORD turned to him and said, "Go in the strength you have and save Israel out of Midian's hand. Am I not sending you?"

"But, LORD," Gideon asked, "how can I save Israel? My clan is the weakest in Manasseh, and I am the least in my family."

The LORD answered, "I will be with you, and you will strike down all the Midianites together." (Judg. 6:12–16)

We need to hear one more conversation. This one is between Jeremiah the prophet and the Lord:

"Before I formed you in the womb I knew you,
 before you were born I set you apart;
 I appointed you as a prophet to the nations."

"Ah, Sovereign Lord," I said, "I do not know how to speak; I am only a child."

But the LORD said to me, "Do not say, 'I am only a child.' You must go to everyone I send you to and say whatever I command you. Do not be afraid of them, for I am with you and will rescue you," declares the LORD. (Jer. 1:5–8)

Do you see yourself in Moses? In Gideon? In Jeremiah? Be encouraged. When Moses obeyed, God made him a great leader and called him "friend." When Gideon obeyed, God used him to free Israel from the Midianites.

When Jeremiah obeyed, God spoke through him warning His people of their disobedience. Moses, Gideon, and Jeremiah—three servants of God were lifted up and given a new and larger vision of God's plan for their lives.

God has always blessed His people by allowing them to serve within His plan when they obey Him. The story of Hudson Taylor whom God called to serve in China is a story of obedience. As a young man, Hudson Taylor knew God was calling him to the mission field, and he prepared well by praying, studying God's Word, and learning the Chinese language. In 1853, when he was only twenty-one years of age, he sailed for China. Years of hardship followed as Westerners were not welcome in China at this time, but God met his every need. He went to regions of China that were untouched by the gospel of Christ Jesus, and God never failed him. Taylor organized the China Inland Mission, bringing more missionaries to the interior. When Hudson Taylor died in 1905, the mission numbered 750 missionaries. We may never know how many people came into God's family because Hudson Taylor was one of God's servants who chose to obey Him.[2]

We find it hard to turn loose of the plans we have for our lives and just obey Jesus when it becomes evident that the Lord has other plans for our lives. We worry and fret and cry out to God. We don't want God to send us to Africa or India or China. We don't want to miss the comfortable life we've planned; sometimes we may try to move into new ministries that look exciting to us without seriously considering where God wants us to serve. If we hold on to our limited vision, we may find ourselves working against God's plan. And that's disobedience. In those times we need to enlarge our vision and remember that a servant seeks God's plan and then obeys.

A Servant Is on Duty Every Day

Jesus did not call us to part-time service. We can't be just Sunday Christians. That does not mean that we must always be busy with our primary ministry—you know, teaching a class at Sunday school or visiting someone in the hospital or counseling a young couple. We are to serve others moment by moment in our homes, in our places of business, in the park, or on a trip—wherever we may be. A friend of mine prays every morning that God will send those across her path that day who need her help. Could it be that everyone we meet during our day is by divine appointment? If we are sensitive to the leading of the Holy Spirit, we will not miss an opportunity to serve.

But do you sometimes forget that you're a servant of the King, and He has plans for your day? I do. Usually it happens when I'm tired or busy or company's coming. Friends going between San Francisco and Los Angeles often stop over at our house for a visit. At other times the church office calls and wants to send special people to be loved and cared for in our home. I'll admit that the Lord has heard me complain a few times about the cleaning of the house when He's sent so many people our way. "Are you forgetting, Lord," I ask, "that I'm the one who will be doing the cleaning after they're gone?" And He answers, "Isn't that what servants are for? To keep My house in order? Have you forgotten that your mission is to serve and love others that they may come to know Me?"

To keep His house in order, to serve, to love—Jesus wants us to have a servant's heart that others may see His love in us. He calls us to let go of our fears and allow Him to lift us up, high above our little worlds. He calls us to a new vision. A vision for His people. A vision for His Church.

Discovering His Plans

1. How do you feel when you are told that you are a "child of the King"? "Chosen"? "Greatly loved"? "Member of God's own family"?

2. Think back over the past decade of your life. Has your vision of God's plan for the world and for your life changed? How?

3. What three things distinguish a servant from one who lives for himself alone? What evidence can you offer that you are a servant of our King?

4. What are some of the reasons we sometimes fail in our efforts to serve Jesus when we serve others?

9

Called to Be His Church

On August 14, 1945, a group of us gathered at the Officers' Club on Almagorda Air Force Base in New Mexico. We knew World War II was drawing to a close and we waited. When the news of a cease-fire came, the room reverberated with shouts of joy.

Then suddenly our attention was drawn to the piano where a young lieutenant struck the first notes of the national anthem. Voices were silenced. We all stood, and with hearts filled with both gladness and sorrow we sang "The Star Spangled Banner."

A few of us slipped quietly out the side door and made our way to the base chapel where twenty or thirty others had already gathered. We felt a strong sense of God's presence as we knelt in prayer to praise and worship Him. My heart was filled with thanksgiving that my husband was kneeling beside me and that he had come home safely.

Kneeling to my left was my friend, Judy, whose husband did not return. Bill's plane went down over Berlin. I remember taking Judy's hand and weeping with her. God's love surrounded us both. A short time later the chaplain rose and led us in worshiping God and ministering to each other. As we prepared to leave, the chaplain reminded us that many others on the base would need our comfort and help in the days to come. We were ready to minister because we had been together as His Church.

The Church of Jesus Christ is Christ's body, believers who have been brought into His family. We are the Church, joined together by our faith in Christ Jesus and the power of His Spirit. We are divided into many local churches meeting in homes, in buildings, in great cathedrals, in big cities and small farm towns, in jungles, mountains, and deserts. Most of our local churches are affiliated with denominations, but we are called to be one body: His Church, the Church universal.

The Church Is Born

Are you as amazed as I am when you read in the Book of Acts that the Church started with only 120 people gathered in the upper room in Jerusalem? One hundred and twenty people! It's even more amazing when we read that their leaders, the twelve Jesus had trained, really didn't understand God's plan. Look what eleven of them asked when Jesus appeared after the resurrection: "'Lord, are you at this time going to restore the kingdom to Israel?'" Jesus' words must have shocked them. "'It is not for you to know the times or dates the Father has set by his own authority. But you will receive power when the Holy Spirit comes on you; and you will be my witnesses in Jerusalem, and in all Judea and Samaria, and to the ends of the earth'" (Acts 1:6–8).

"To the ends of the earth!" That was a big assignment, but not too big for God. When the Holy Spirit fell on those 120 believers, they were filled with power, confidence, and compassion. They declared the "wonders of

God." They held up Jesus. They worshiped Him. They knew He was the Christ, the Son of the living God.

In his first sermon, Peter laid out God's plan for all who would listen. Now he saw the plan clearly. He understood what God had been telling His people all along: "'I will pour out my Spirit on all people. . . . And everyone who calls on the name of the Lord will be saved'" (Acts 2:17, 21). Three thousand people were added to the church that day, and as the believers spread the good news, the number grew to five thousand. Then more. And more. . . .

Today, out of a reported 1994 world population of 5,642,000,000 people, almost half claim to be Christians—members of His kingdom, His family, His Church. The number may be even higher; many church authorities will not release the numbers of members in their denominations. New believers are added. Others fall away. New churches are organized daily. Churches join together.

However, with all this growth, I have some concerns. I remember how excited those 120 charter members must have been over the phenomenal growth of the church during the first century. Then, I read the words of Jesus in the Book of Revelation. He appeared to John and evaluated His Church about sixty years after its beginning. The numbers were there. Local congregations were scattered over the known world. There was praise for many things, but the Church was judged severely for the things that are important to God and His plan.

Jesus Speaks to His Church

The chart on pages 110–11, based on Revelation 2–3, will be helpful to us as we have a look at the concerns Jesus had for His Church in the first century. He saw the hearts of His people and knew the inner workings of each of the seven congregations. Together these seven churches symbolize the Church universal, and what Jesus had to say to these ancient people has been preserved in His Word for the Church today.

There is always perfect order in everything God does. In the evaluation of the seven churches, Jesus followed the order of praise, judgment, warning, and promise. There is no praise for the churches at Sardis and Laodicea, and no judgment of Smyrna and Philadelphia, but there is warning and promise for all seven.

Praise

Let's consider the seven churches as one and make a list of the things the church was doing that pleased Jesus—things which brought praise, things that He would surely praise us for today:

- Working hard.
- Persevering; no complaining.
- Testing false teachers.
- Enduring hardships for the sake of Jesus' name.
- Rich in spiritual things.
- Remaining true to Jesus.
- Increasing service.
- Loving.
- Faithful.
- Obedient.

It sounds as if the church was doing everything right. This must have been true for many believers who were a part of the fellowships in the first century. The apostles were faithfully serving Jesus. So were people like Barnabas, Timothy, Lydia, Silas, Aquila, and Priscilla. Many believers today are earnestly striving to live lives pleasing to the Lord. They are disciples working within His plan, helping to build His Church.

	Ephesus	Smyrna	Pergamum	Thyatira
Praise	"I know your deeds, your hard work and your perseverance. I know that you cannot tolerate wicked men, that you have tested those who claim to be apostles but are not, and found them false. You have persevered and have endured hardships for my name, and have not grown weary" (2:2–3).	"I know your afflictions and your poverty—yet you are rich" (2:9).	"I know where you live—where Satan has his throne. Yet you remain true to my name. You did not renounce your faith in me" (2:13).	"I know your deeds, your love and faith, your service and perseverance, and that you are now doing more than you did at first" (2:19).
Judgment	"You have forsaken your first love" (2:4).		"You have people there who hold to the teaching of Balaam, . . . Likewise you also have those who hold to the teaching of the Nicolaitans" (2:14–15).	"You tolerate that woman Jezebel. . . . By her teaching she misleads my servants into sexual immorality and the eating of food sacrificed to idols" (2:20).
Warning	"Remember the height from which you have fallen! Repent and do the things you did at first. If you do not repent, I will come to you and remove your lampstand" (2:5).	"Do not be afraid of what you are about to suffer. I tell you, the devil will put some of you in prison to test you, and you will suffer persecution for ten days" (2:10a).	"Repent therefore! Otherwise, I will soon come to you and will fight against them [those who hold to false teaching] with the sword of my mouth" (2:16).	"I will make those who commit adultery with her suffer intensely, unless they repent of her ways. . . . I will repay each of you according to your deeds. . . . Hold on to what you have until I come" (2:21–25).
Promise	"To him who overcomes, I will give the right to eat from the tree of life, which is in the paradise of God" (2:7).	"Be faithful, even to the point of death, and I will give you the crown of life. . . . He who overcomes will not be hurt by the second death" (2:10–11).	"To him who overcomes I will give some of the hidden manna. I will also give him a white stone with a new name written on it" (2:17).	"To him who overcomes and does my will to the end, I will give authority over the nations. . . . I will also give him the morning star" (2:26–28.)

	Sardis	Philadelphia	Laodicea
Praise		"I know that you have little strength, yet you have kept my word, and have not denied my name. . . . You have kept my command to endure patiently" (3:8,10).	
Judgment	"I know your deeds; you have a reputation of being alive, but you are dead" (3:1).		"I know your deeds, that you are neither cold nor hot" (3:15).
Warning	"Wake up! Strengthen what remains and is about to die. . . . Remember, therefore, what you have received and heard; obey it; and repent. But if you do not wake up, I will come like a thief, and you will not know at what time I will come to you" (3:2-3).	"Hold on to what you have, so that no one will take your crown" (3:11).	"I counsel you to buy from me gold refined in the fire, so you can become rich; and white clothes to wear so you can cover your shameful nakedness; and salve to put on your eyes so you can see. . . . So be earnest and repent" (3:18-19).
Promise	"Yet you have a few people in Sardis who have not soiled their clothes. They will walk with me, dressed in white, for they are worthy. He who overcomes will, like them, be dressed in white. I will never blot out his name from the book of life, but will acknowledge his name before my Father and his angels" (3:4-5).	"I will keep you from the hour of trial that is going to come upon the whole world. . . . Him who overcomes I will make a pillar in the temple of my God. Never again will he leave it. I will write on him the name of my God and the name of the city of my God . . . and I will also write on him my new name" (3:10-12).	"Here I am! I stand at the door and knock. If anyone hears my voice and opens the door, I will come in and eat with him, and he with me. To him who overcomes. I will give the right to sit with me on my throne, just as I overcame and sat down with my Father on his throne" (3:20-22).

Judgment

Jesus had more to say to that early church. Not everything was perfect. Let's list the things found in some of those early congregations that did not please Him:

- Jesus was no longer their first love; they had wrong priorities.
- Some believers held to false teaching.
- Some practiced immorality and caused others to stumble.
- Immoral people were tolerated in the congregation.
- Deeds made them appear to be alive, but they were dead.
- Believers were lukewarm—neither hot nor cold.

That's rather severe judgment for many first-century Christians. But what about the Church today? The Church of Jesus Christ in the twentieth century? Are we guilty of the same sins—or worse? In 1982, David Watson wrote, "We live today in a sick church that desperately needs God's healing."[1] Ten years later Chuck Colson argued in his book, *The Body*, that the Church is in an identity crisis. He feels that Christians have been "sucked in by the radical individualism of secular culture and the soothing sermons of the feel-good gospel. Many have sold out to a consumer-oriented McChurch mentality."[2]

There is no lack of books pointing out what is wrong with the church today. In his book *Dining with the Devil*, Os Guinness argues that the megachurch movement is flirting dangerously with modernity. In *A Church for the 21st Century*, author Leith Anderson warns that yesterday's successes are no guarantee of tomorrow's survival. Another writer, Raymond Ortlund, pleads with us to "let the church be the church" in his book by that name.

My concerns deepen when I read surveys with conclusions like these:

The majority of born-again Christians and people who attend evangelical churches agree with the statement that Christians, Jews, Buddhists, and others pray to the same god but simply use different names for that deity.

Within the Christian community, the majority believe that Satan is simply a symbol of evil, and not actually a living being or spirit.

Only 43 percent of evangelical Christians believe that they have any responsibility for sharing their beliefs with others.[3]

Not long ago, *Christianity Today* reported that an Episcopalian bishop took his own life after being involved in adulterous relationships, and an evangelical minister who conducted the funeral of an AIDS activist was vilified by homosexual activists and the secular press for discussing eternal salvation at the service.[4] During the past decade several well-known television evangelists have fallen from God's plan, overcome by greed and desire for the things of the world.

Warning

Jesus had some words of warning for His Church that we will do well to hear today. Let's make another list.

- Remember, repent, and return to your first love.
- Don't fear suffering, prison, or even death.
- Beware of false teachers. You will be held responsible for the Word.
- Immoral conduct will bring suffering and judgment.
- Obey, repent, and grow strong spiritually.
- Cling to the truth that you have.
- Be earnest, sincere in repentance.

These warnings are clearly applicable today both to the church and to us as individual believers. We must stand firm and ask the Holy Spirit to strengthen our faith. We have the promise of the One who rules heaven and earth that His plan and His Church will not fail. When Peter faced his Master and declared, "'You are the Christ, the Son of the living God,'" Jesus said, "'On this rock I will build my church, and the gates of Hades will not overcome it'" (Matt. 16:16, 18). Peter's words may be the rock Jesus was referring to, or the rock could be Peter himself. (See Eph. 2:20.) Both interpretations are significant, but the definitive message in Jesus' promise is that *the Church will not fail*. Satan will not overcome the Church which Jesus Himself is building.

Promise

Jesus' words should encourage us. He is still Head of His Church. He knows His people. He will bring us through victoriously. Jesus has more promises for us—rewards for following the plan He has for His Church. Here's another list! Read it and be encouraged:

- We will eat from the tree of life—have eternal life.

- We will receive the crown of life.

- He will feed us from His Word, and we will know Him as no one else does. He will make us victorious.

- We will have the Morning Star, Jesus Himself.

- We will be pure because we belong to Jesus who will be our advocate before the Father. Our name will be written in the Book of Life.

- Jesus will keep us from the hour of trial that is coming on the Church. We will be pillars in God's temple where we will dwell forever as His family.

- If we ask, Jesus will help us. If we allow Him to come into our hearts, we will rule with Him someday.

Our look at Jesus' evaluation of His Church, as John recorded it in the Book of Revelation, has been brief. But has it made you aware of how deeply concerned Jesus is about His plan for the growth of His people, the building of His Church? It has me. In John's vision Jesus was standing in the midst of the Church. He saw everything His people were doing. Perhaps we would do things differently in our local churches and in our lives if we believed the truth that Jesus sees all that we do. He knows our hearts—our thoughts. He's counting on us to work with Him in building His Church. We are to *be* His Church.

Three Priorities for the Church

Jesus modeled His plan for building the Church during those three years He walked the earth. He clearly set three priorities: (1) the Father; (2) the disciples; (3) the world.

As I think back on that memorable experience I had with the Church in the little base chapel in Almagorda, I realize that when I entered the white frame building with its cross reaching to the heavens, I just wanted to worship God. To be with Him. To talk to Him. To listen. Then after awhile, Judy's quiet weeping drew me to her and to others around me as we joined together to sing praises, to hear the chaplain read God's Word, and to minister to each other. When we left the chapel, we were prepared to carry out God's command to reach out to others and fulfill our mission. It was Jesus' model: First, God. Next, the family of believers. Then, the world.

Let me suggest three priorities for the church which follow the pattern of Jesus' ministry.

Worship God and Enjoy His Fellowship

Jesus kept in close fellowship with the Father. Luke reminds us: "Jesus often withdrew to lonely places and prayed" (5:16). "One of those days Jesus went out to a mountainside to pray, and spent the night praying to God" (6:12). "Once when Jesus was praying in private and his disciples were with him" (9:18). "One day Jesus was praying in a certain place" (11:1).

Note where Jesus was when He spent this special time with the Father: "lonely places," "mountainside," "private," or "certain place." The first three remind us to spend time daily in fellowship and communion with our Lord. Jesus did. And if Jesus needed that quiet time with God, we certainly do. Then, that "certain place" reminds me that Jesus must have had a place where He often went to be with the Father. I'm not at all sure that it was the synagogue, although he often went there, but I believe that for us that "certain place" should include the local church where we go to worship on Sundays.

Our God is a holy God, and coming into His presence is a sacred and holy occasion. It is a time to fall before Him in worship, in praise, and in thanksgiving. The Westminster Shorter Catechism states, "Man's chief end is to glorify God, and to enjoy him forever." I find that after I've greeted friends at the door of my church on Sundays, I want to enter into a quiet sanctuary and spend a few moments with my Lord before the worship service begins. I just want to say, "Lord, I sense Your presence. Your beauty. Your holiness. I want to bow before You, to worship You, because You alone are my Lord. Make my heart ready for this time of fellowship with You and with my church family in Your Church."

We do not always have these few minutes of private time with our Lord before the worship service begins, however. Most often we are led into God's presence by the worship leader who through Scripture, song, and prayer, draws us to see God, that we may worship Him. Either way, these few minutes prepare us for all that is to follow. They focus our attention on our God. They are important.

Do you know what John did when he saw Jesus in all His glory standing before Him surrounded by the Church? John "fell at his feet as though dead" (Rev. 1:17). Later John was taken up to heaven in the Spirit, to the very throne of God, and saw all the radiance and majesty of the One we worship. He heard those gathered around the throne singing, "Holy, holy, holy is the Lord God Almighty, who was, and is, and is to come" (Rev. 4:8). This is the God we serve and worship. We are His Church. And we are called to bow our hearts before Him in reverence and praise as we enjoy His fellowship.

Equip Believers and Care for Each Other

Paul explained one of the most important reasons for the local church to exist: "It was he who gave some to be apostles, some to be prophets, some to be evangelists, and some to be pastors and teachers, to prepare God's people for works of service, so that the body of Christ may be built up until we all reach unity in the faith and in the knowledge of the Son of God and become mature, attaining to the whole measure of the fullness of Christ" (Eph. 4:11–13).

Does your church emphasize education? Many don't. But I believe in education from the cradle roll through senior adults. There are many things that we need to learn within the fellowship of other believers. We need their input and their support.

Chuck Colson shares this view in his book *The Body*: "The church must do everything it can to equip believers with an understanding of Scripture, of doctrine, and of the application of Christian truth to all of life. . . . Make no mistake. Failure to teach is a betrayal of the Great Commission. And it is dangerous."[5]

It is dangerous indeed. We need well-trained teachers. Sunday school classes. Small study groups. Seminars. Workshops. Our worship services are vitally important, but if we neglect the training of believers, our Lord might well say to us as He did to the people of Hosea's time, "My people are destroyed from lack of knowledge" (4:6).

Not only must we equip believers, but we must care for each other. This means ministering to the needs of those in our community of believers in whatever ways are helpful. Several years ago a member of our church board lost his job and was about to lose his home. He could not make the payments. The board took an offering among themselves and made the payments until he got a job in another city and sold his home. A few months later a check arrived to cover the amount he was given. The board used the money to start a We Care fund and made it available for others who might need temporary help. Thrift shops, food pantries, volunteers to take in meals when needed and to care for those who are ill, volunteer drivers, shoppers—all these are vital ministries. They are His Church in action, lovingly caring for each other. Oftentimes we forget that all someone needs is our presence or a kind word.

We go to church forgetting that we are to minister as well as be ministered to. A friend of mine told me of a time when she learned this truth. One rainy Sunday morning Jenny was tempted to stay home. She was bored with many things in her church, especially the pastor's sermons, and she could see no real reason for going. Her husband was excited about ushering that morning, so she said nothing. Later as she read the bulletin while waiting for the service to begin, she noted that the same names appeared on the prayer list. *Does Susie Miller expect us to pray about her arthritis all year long?* she wondered. *And why does Greg Wallace need a new job? If he'd work a little harder he'd be able to keep the one he has.* The pastor's sermon watered Jenny's resentment. *Pastor must not spend any time at all in preparation for his sermon,* she thought.

When the pastor gave the benediction and the organ began the postlude, Jenny gathered up her raincoat, purse, and Bible and started toward the side door of the sanctuary. She was anxious to get home. Her husband stopped to greet Mrs. Benson, a tiny little lady seated in front of them who didn't look as if she weighed more than a hundred pounds. "Let me help you with your coat, Mrs. Benson," he said. "It's all wet. Surely you didn't walk those six blocks to church in this rain!"

Jenny caught Mrs. Benson's smile as she said, "Oh my, yes, I did! I wouldn't miss morning worship with all you dear friends for anything. You're all the family I have, you know, and I only see you on Sundays."

"You're a real inspiration to me, Mrs. Benson," Jenny's husband said. "Not many people are as faithful as you."

Tears rolled down Jenny's face as Mrs. Benson reached over and touched both their arms. "God bless both of you dear people. Sometimes I don't think I'm giving anything to my family—just taking so much from all of you. My, wasn't that a good sermon? Pastor's words stay with me all week. I'm learning so much about our wonderful Lord."

Jenny smiled through her tears as she gave Mrs. Benson a big hug. Then she reached for her purse and walked with her special friend to the front door. She didn't want to miss greeting Pastor.

Reach Out to the World and Fulfill His Plan

I wonder if we as individuals are doing all that we should to fulfill our mission in reaching the world around us. I know Jesus calls many people to take the gospel message to those who live in foreign lands; but I believe Jesus would also agree with the old saying, "Bloom where you are planted." For most of us the road to Samaria leads right through our neighborhoods. And that means caring for those God has placed within our touch in a variety of ways. Jesus healed the sick, comforted those in sorrow, and fed the hungry. Most importantly, He taught them about God's plan to save all who would come to Him, and He promised them eternal life. At the same time He trained the disciples to follow in His footsteps. Then, He sent them out to minister under the power of the Spirit.

Remember Jesus' words to the disciples just before He ascended to heaven? "'Go and make disciples of all nations, baptizing them in the name of the Father and of the Son and of the Holy Spirit, and teaching them to obey everything I have commanded you. And surely I am with you always, to the very end of the age'" (Matt. 28:19–20).

That's God's plan. Someone told us about Jesus, discipled us, gave us the desire to be baptized, and taught us to obey God's Word. As we do the same for those in our mission field, we are His disciples, empowered by the Holy Spirit to fulfill His plan for the Church.

I was troubled when I read in Russell Chandler's book *Racing Toward 2001* about the work the Muslims are doing right in our neighborhoods: "Islamic mosques are being built by the hundreds throughout the U.S., and Islamic teachings are being propogated vigorously. . . . Lawud Assad, president of the Council of Mosques of the United States, says there are more than 1,000 Muslim community organizations in his group alone, some worshiping in basements and other make shift places."[6]

Did you know that the second largest religious group in our world is the Muslims, who claim 1,869,751,000 worshipers? The Mormon church also shows spectacular growth. Chandler reports that in 1989 alone, this group "baptized 393,940 people into the faith, or an average of 1,082 every day!"[7]

What can we do? How can we reach those God has put in our paths? Where can we find the courage to be His disciples in ministry to our neighborhood?

I remember well when we first moved into the neighborhood we live in now. I didn't know anyone who lived within a six-block radius of our home. I thought about visiting around the neighborhood many times, but I hid behind the excuses of "They're never at home," or "I don't want to intrude," or "They have their own friends." If it was my mission field, I was depending on the media to beam the story of Jesus into my neighbors' homes or to send it via the mailman.

The idea of reaching my neighbors for Christ was a bit frightening. I thought of the apostle Paul who was fearless in telling people about Jesus. I asked God to give me a loving heart, a heart deeply concerned for my neighbors. To help me become better acquainted with my neighbors, I began to invite them to our home—two couples at a time. This led to desserts that included five or six couples. Then we had a family barbecue. Eventually, these invitations led to a neighborhood Bible study and the opportunity to share the love of Jesus.

When our first Bible study was well established, we joined with another couple from our church and invited our neighbors to hear Dave Hanna, founder of Athletes in Action. Out of that evening came five Bible studies—all in our neighborhood. Today, twenty of our neighbors meet in our home on Thursday evenings to study God's Word.

Housing our neighbors' overflow guests has been another way of reaching out in ministry. A Bible and Christian magazines on a bedside table, a prayer of thanks before a meal, a cup of hot tea served at bedtime—all these show our love of God. They provide an extra bonus to helping our neighbors.

Of course, your neighborhood may not be your primary ministry. God may ask you to minister to the workers in your office or place of business. To your children's friends. To those living in a convalescent care center. The list of mission fields for most towns today is endless. If you are serious about being a disciple of Jesus Christ, He will place you where you can be used to help build His Church.

We are blessed, greatly blessed. We are called to *be* His Church. We can know the joy of close communion with our God as we worship and praise Him. We can know the strength and loving fellowship of believers as we share the lives of those in His Church, and we can be a part of His plan as we reach out to the world in ministry that others may come to know Jesus.

Discovering His Plans

1. What amazes you most about the 120 people who gathered in the upper room?

2. Look over the list of praises Jesus had for His Church about sixty years after His Spirit came upon those in the upper room. Are these ten characteristics true of your local body of believers? Are they true of you personally?

3. Consider the six judgments Jesus made on His Church. Which ones do you think are relevant for the Church today? How do you feel about David Watson's comment that the Church today "desperately needs God's healing"?

4. Jesus gave seven warnings to the early church. Explain specifically how these warnings apply to His Church and to us personally today.

5. How do you feel knowing that the seven promises Jesus gave to His Church in the first century are also for us today? Are you encouraged?

6. Do you agree with the three priorities for the church: (a) worship God and enjoy His fellowship; (b) equip believers and care for each other; and (c) reach out to the world and fulfill His plan? If so, then how can your spiritual gifts be used to advance them?

10

Called to Freedom

I remember the day my dad took me to the University of Texas. I was a young teenager, eager to try my wings away from home. As we approached the administration building and started up the steps, Dad stopped and pointed to the words carved in stone above the door. "You shall know the truth, and the truth shall set you free." He turned to me with a serious expression on his face. "Every time you walk through those doors," he said, "remind yourself that that promise comes with a stipulation: '*If* you hold to my teaching . . . .'" He turned and made a wide sweep of the campus with his hand. "All the learning taking place in these buildings, all the books in that library over there, will not give you the truth or set you free. Only Jesus can do that. He *is* the truth."

I've thought about Dad's words many times over the years, especially after I became a military wife. You hear a lot about freedom in the military. Our forces joined with the people of England, France, and the Netherlands in their fight for freedom back in the 1940s. Later our concern shifted to the Koreans, the Vietnamese, and the Cambodians. More recently our sympathy has gone out to the Cuban and Haitian refugees fleeing from their homelands in search of freedom. Struggles for freedom go on today in Africa, South America, Europe, Asia—around the world.

Even in our own American country we hear this cry for freedom. The NAACP and the Civil Liberties Union came into being because deep in the hearts of our people is a yearning to be free. The cry is not just to be free in the public arena. It is also heard in the private sector of our lives. Just a short time ago a beloved member of our church congregation said to his wife, "I'm moving out. You and the children are smothering me. I just want to be free." This is no isolated case. This yearning for freedom is breaking up homes all over America.

Where will the search for freedom end? Many who seek to be free will find they are running after a mirage. As important as it is to be free from the tyranny of dictators, the tyranny of prejudice, oppression, and poverty—all these are temporary, material. Dad knew that.

As believers, we may be tempted to agree with the pompous Jews who said to Jesus, "We've never been slaves to anyone!" Not so! Jesus pointed out that "'everyone who sins is a slave to sin'" (John 8:33–34). Being a slave of sin is not being free. But if we are believers, Jesus has freed us from this bondage. He broke sin's hold on us, called us into His family, and set us free to be His disciples.

Coming into God's family, free in Christ Jesus, also means that we are free to choose whether or not we will allow the Holy Spirit to mold us and teach us and guide us. Only in choosing to obey can we be made free in every area of our lives—free to serve Jesus and fulfill our assignment in God's plan.

I love the Book of Exodus because I learn so much from it. Every time I read it I marvel at God's patience with a people who struggled so hard against being free. God freed them from slavery in Egypt, yet when life got a little rough out in the desert, they cried to go back to Egypt. He freed them from the worship of false gods, yet they made a golden calf and worshiped it. They weren't satisfied with the freedom God gave them.

Not only do we have these examples before us, but we have the promise of Jesus: "'If you hold to my teaching, you are really my disciples. Then you will know the truth, and the truth will set you free. . . . So if the Son sets you free, you will be free indeed'" (John 8:31–32, 36). Why, then, do we block our freedom to really *live*? Why are we afraid to live on the growing edge? Why do we hesitate to turn over every area of our lives to Jesus Christ?

I believe there are a number of reasons. It seems to me that they all stem from fear—a response Jesus condemned as the opposite of faith. Let's look at four fears that can hold us in bondage, fears that keep us from being free to become all that Jesus wants us to become.

Fear of Being a Fanatic

I remember one night when my son's high school youth group met at our home. I listened in and was surprised to hear "Praise the Lord," "Thank You, Jesus," and other expressions of real joy. I know now that this was a committed group of teenagers, but at the time I was sure that Rick was becoming a fanatic, and I didn't know how to handle it. Every time I tried to pray about Rick, the Lord said to me, "It's not Rick I'm concerned about. I want to talk about you." I needed help. Although I had many Christian friends at the time, strangely enough I turned to the only friend I had whom I classified as a "fanatic" for Jesus Christ. Marian was not afraid to talk about Jesus. She was comfortable talking about Him because she walked so close to Him. I had no doubt about where she stood.

Do you enjoy talking to others about Jesus? Are you comfortable using the name of Jesus in front of your friends who are not believers? Do you find it easy to offer to pray with someone who comes to you with a problem? If your answer to all these questions is yes, then I doubt that you're afraid to share what Jesus has done for you. If your answer is no, then beware. Failure to speak when the Spirit bids us speak not only leads us into disobedience but can cause us to deny our Lord. We should not invent situations, but rather we should feel free to express our views—to lovingly share something that has proven to be true for us. We should never be afraid to live on the growing edge.

Fear of What Friends Will Think

I've found this fear to be unfounded. I recall with shame the many times on the Allan Hancock College campus, where I taught for a number of years, when I failed to express my worldview—my philosophy of life centered in Christ Jesus. My colleagues freely expressed theirs, but a gnawing fear deep inside me kept me from sharing what Jesus had done in my life. I'm thankful that through the help of the Holy Spirit I overcame this fear. I now speak freely because I know I have the answer. I have the truth, and my friends need to know.

We are the salt of the earth, the light in a dark world. Jesus has placed each of us in the midst of many who do not know Him. But, you may be asking, how can I find the freedom to tell my unbelieving friends about Jesus? Here are three suggestions to help you overcome the fear of what you imagine your friends will think.

First, read some good books on friendship evangelism. There are many good ones on the market. You might want to have a look at *Out of Their Faces and into Their Shoes* by John Kramp, *Out of the Salt Shaker* by Becky Pippert, *The Master Plan of Evangelism* by Robert E. Coleman, or *Gentle Persuasion* by Joseph C. Aldrich.

Second, maintain close friendships with some non-Christians. Be available to join them for lunch or to help with a project in which they are interested. Take the initiative and invite them to your home often.

Third, invite both Christian and non-Christian friends to participate together in some of the activities they both enjoy. I once issued a blanket invitation to my English class to join our InterVarsity group for a retreat in the mountains one weekend. I told them that if they had never studied the Bible they should at least find out if there was any truth in it. "After all," I said, "it's some of the greatest literature ever written." Several of the students went with us and heard about Jesus.

Who is going to tell our friends about Jesus if we fail them?

Fear of What Jesus Will Do

Does this one sound strange to you? There was a time in my life when it was a real concern to me—not for what Jesus might ask me to do for Him, but what He might want to do with my children. Have you ever faced a situation when you were sure you knew better than God what would make your child's life meaningful? I have. I remember how upset I was when our son, Rick, announced that he was getting married following his freshman year in college. He and Syndi had met at Hume Lake Christian Camp three years earlier when their high school youth groups were there on retreat, but we thought they were too young. We couldn't understand why Rick couldn't finish college first. Surely God didn't approve of their timing! Yet we were sure Syndi's family was praying just as hard as we were. After the wedding the young couple returned to college, and today they live only twenty miles from us. They are right for each other—and God knew it before we did.

I wish I could say I learned from God's care of my son that He would also care for my daughter Connie, but I didn't. I was at Regent College in Vancouver one summer when Connie called to tell me she was entering pilot training. She was an air force nurse, caring for the sick and comforting the hurting. I was proud of her. My reaction to her news was anything but pleasing to the Lord. "God, why are you doing this to me? I don't want her to fly! Don't you know it's dangerous?" I'm thankful that Connie listened to God. Over the past few years I have seen God's wisdom as He has matured Connie in her faith and given her a ministry in the military that she could never have had if she had not followed God's plan.

The more we trust the Lord with the lives of our children, the more exciting all our lives become. He removes the fear of what lies ahead. We begin to see Him at work in our children's lives and realize the wisdom of His plan.

What about trusting Him with our life's work? That's not easy—not when we love what we're doing. I had been on church staff as director of adult ministries for three years when the Lord moved me out of this ministry into a full-time ministry of writing—and it was a difficult move for me. I loved the people of my church. They were growing in the Lord, excited, eager to learn. A large majority were using their gifts in vibrant ministries. I hung on tightly, working at the church part-time for several months while trying to write at the same time. Although I'm sure the Lord understood that I needed this time of transition, I'm not sure it was His first plan for me.

During a quiet time at a writers' conference, the Spirit led me to a verse in God's Word which helped me to turn loose and trust the Lord to direct my life: "'Unless a kernel of wheat falls to the ground and dies, it remains only a single seed. But if it dies, it produces many seeds'" (John 12:24). Once again the Lord was right. It has been a slow process for me, but I have learned not to fear His plan for my life.

Fear of Being Inadequate

When we know that we are called to a certain ministry, I'm not sure we should ever feel inadequate. The power of the God who created the universe and holds the fate of nations in His hand is enough to enable us to do any task. If we are believers, we have God's Spirit within us!

God is not looking just for people with two college degrees to do His work. He is looking for those with hearts and wills totally yielded to Him. He is looking for those who believe that He does indeed work in and through us. He is looking for those who each morning are able to say, "Lord, I'm available. I wonder what you have for me to do today!" It's exciting to be free—to live on the growing edge.

I'll never forget the day Esther Herriott signed up for my workshop in teacher training. She had never taught before and was sure that she wasn't gifted in that area. She made it clear to me that she was only taking the course because her husband, Jud, wanted to teach and had persuaded her to come with him. At the end of the workshop, I videotaped each person teaching a short lesson, and Esther was outstanding! But nothing I could say would convince her that God had given her the gift of teaching.

Esther and Jud taught a Sunday school class together—with Jud doing the major part of the teaching. Then the Lord began to work in Esther's life. She got excited about the Bible and spent hours daily studying it. When that happens, you have to share with others what God is teaching you! When I started teaching a class designed to take students through the Old Testament, Esther agreed to help me. At the end of a few weeks, she took over the class of more than a hundred people! God takes our inadequacies and makes us adequate if we are willing to do our part and to trust Him for the rest.

One more story will show you how exciting this life can be if we are free to live on the growing edge. Not long ago I went with my daughter-in-law to Los Angeles to take care of some business. That morning I said to the Lord, "You know I'm going to the big city today, and I doubt if You have anything for me to do that's special—but I'm available!"

I had to wait at the courthouse for Syndi for two hours, so I walked around the grounds, enjoying the rest and enduring the heat. I noticed a little old lady slowly making her way up the steep stairs to the courthouse and offered to help her. I asked where she was going and she told me the Social Security office. She was unsure where the office was, so I suggested that she wait there for me while I went inside to inquire. I ran ahead, made the inquiries, and discovered that the office wasn't in this building at all. It was in another building across the block. I returned to my new friend and offered to walk with her to her destination.

"Now isn't that nice of the Lord?" she said. "I told Him when I started out this morning that I would need some help today, and here He's sent you!" She was eighty-one years old and had traveled by bus across the city. I spent the entire two hours with her and was concerned about her taking the bus home alone.

Just at that moment, a neighbor of my new friend's walked up and said, "Oh, Mrs. Jordan, what a surprise to see you here! When you're ready to go home, I'll take you." A smile crossed my friend's face. "See," she said, patting my arm, "you don't have to worry about me. The Lord's got everything worked out for my day."

Yes, Jesus calls us to freedom. He wants us to live exciting lives free from bondage to this world, free to serve Him.

We don't have to fear being a fanatic. We're just more excited about Jesus and His plan than anything else!

We don't have to fear what our friends will think. We have the answers to their questions. If they're searching for freedom, we know they will find it only in Jesus.

We don't have to fear what Jesus will do in the lives of our children or others close to us. He has every hair of their heads numbered and every day of their lives planned.

We don't have to fear changing our job or starting a new ministry or any problem that lies ahead.

We don't have to fear being inadequate. Our God is adequate. He will provide everything we need to serve Him in any ministry to which He calls us.

It is indeed exciting to be free to live on the growing edge. But we cannot forget the key to our freedom: "If you hold to my teaching . . . . " God's plan is available to us if we want to escape the bondage of the world and move into the freedom of serving Christ, to grow in Him until the attributes of Christ Jesus can clearly be seen in us. If this is the freedom we seek, it will cost us everything.

As His disciples, our bodies will often be weary as we are led into sacrificial service for our King. Our minds will be transformed by God's Spirit that we may know the truth in Christ Jesus. Our spirits will be led into closer and closer communion with the One who loves us so much. We will be free indeed!

Discovering His Plans

Consider the following problems and evaluate your response:

1. An unbelieving friend comes to you with questions about God. She is interested in finding out how you became a Christian and how she may come to know Jesus.

- Do you feel (a) comfortable, (b) unsure, (c) fearful?
- How would Jesus want you to respond?

2. A neighbor whose life is centered in the world has lost her newborn baby boy. You know that she needs God's

comfort, but you're not sure how she might respond to your offer to pray for her.

- Do you feel (a) comfortable, (b) unsure, (c) fearful?
- How would Jesus want you to respond?

3. You are busy doing things within your church, but you live in a neighborhood of unbelievers. Your pastor suggests that you start a neighborhood Bible study.

- Do you feel (a) comfortable, (b) unsure, (c) fearful?
- How would Jesus want you to respond?

4. You have lost your job and the only new job offer requires that you leave friends and church family and move many miles away to a big city.

- Do you feel (a) comfortable, (b) unsure, (c) fearful?
- How would Jesus want you to respond?

5. The Sunday school superintendent in your church is moving. You are asked to take the position. You have been teaching Sunday school for years, and you have free time.

- Do you feel (a) comfortable, (b) unsure, (c) fearful?
- How would Jesus want you to respond?

6. You know that your spiritual gifts are mercy and encouragement. For the past year you have been going with a strong, mature Christian to visit the sick, comfort those in mourning, and bring encouragement to many experiencing difficulties. Now your teacher wants you to stand alone and take an understudy—to teach another person all you have learned.

- Do you feel (a) comfortable, (b) unsure, (c) fearful?
- How would Jesus want you to respond?

Part 3
The Response of His Children

11

Called to Return

Ann Bailey was one of the busiest people in our church. She was the executive type—dependable and energetic. Everyone admired her. That's why I was surprised when I walked into the adult education office one day and found her crying. Ann quickly grabbed a tissue, lifted her head high, and tried to smile.

"OK. What's the problem?" I asked. "I've never seen you cry before."

Ann's shoulders dropped, and she hesitated only a second before the words came tumbling out. "I've taught Sunday school here for years," she said. "This past year I feel like I'm repeating the same old story—nothing new, exciting. No one in my class is interested. I guess I understand how they feel because I don't even enjoy the worship service anymore. Frankly, it bores me." She rose and walked over to the window. When she turned back to me her face showed the pain she was feeling. "You know I work hard for this church," she said. "I teach. Sing in the choir. Head the Women's Association. Work with Prison

Fellowship. I've never said no to anything I've been asked to do. Why is there no longer joy in my ministry?"

Can you identify with Ann? I can. If we are active in our church and committed to serving Jesus in ministry, most of us will share Ann's dilemma at one time or another. Her problem is not unique—and it's not new. It happened in the church at Ephesus. Jesus identified the problem, and He had a solution.

The Problem

Ephesus was the largest and wealthiest city of Asia. Here all the roads of the province converged to take advantage of the city's great harbor. The city had a large market, magnificent buildings, and gift shops. On the side of a mountain was an amphitheater which seated more than 45,000 people. The temple of Diana and temples honoring Claudius and Nero housed hundreds of sacred prostitutes and were centers of corruption and immorality. Ephesus, like many of our large cities of the world today, was a pagan city. At times the city had as many as two million people who needed to know Jesus. This meant that the church at Ephesus had much work to do.

Paul loved the people in the church at Ephesus. He spent more time with them than with believers in any other church. They were well taught and trained not only by Paul but by John, Timothy, Priscilla, Aquila, and Apollos. John was their pastor for many years—until he was exiled to the Isle of Patmos.

The Christians at Ephesus worked hard. When Jesus appeared to John on Patmos about A.D. 95, He praised them for their diligence. Look what He said: "I know your deeds, your hard work and your perseverance. I know that you cannot tolerate wicked men, that you have tested those who claim to be apostles but are not, and have found them false. You have persevered and have endured hardships for my name, and have not grown weary" (Rev. 2:2–3).

I imagine that believers in this church spent many hours on the Sabbath worshiping God, teaching, and counseling each other. During the week they stayed busy meeting in small groups for teaching, visiting the sick, and ministering to each other in various ways. In their spare time they were busy telling everyone around them about Jesus, patiently enduring the persecution and hardships that this ministry brought about. There were not many pew-sitters in the church at Ephesus.

Does the work of active believers in the church at Ephesus sound very different from the experience of many believers in the church today? If anything, we move at an even faster pace than first-century Christians. Our culture demands it. We somehow feel that we have to keep up or get lost in the shuffle, and this trend has forced its way into the life of the church. We want to be successful in any task we undertake, so we work harder and harder. Soon we gain a reputation for doing things well and for being dependable. Success often means that we are asked to start another ministry, form another committee, organize another fund raiser, or plan another dinner. Tasks are added to tasks, and before long the responsibilities are more than we can handle.

There's nothing wrong with hard work. Paul wrote, "If a man will not work, he shall not eat" (2 Thess. 3:10). Not only are we to work to support our physical well being and that of our families, but we are to work in the special ministries for which the Spirit has equipped us. Certainly we are to obey God's commands and do the work He planned for His Church. There is much work to do, and Jesus warned that "night is coming, when no one can work" (John 9:4). How then can the work we do for the Lord sometimes become meaningless? The danger lies in our focus. Unless we are careful, the work itself may become our focus; but God's plan is that our focus be on Him, that our time with Him be our first priority.

In the early church, all work was far more integrated with the life of the church than it is today. In the Book of Acts, we get a picture of what life was like at the beginning of the church: "All the believers were together and had everything in common. Selling their possessions and goods, they gave to anyone as he had need. Every day they continued to meet together in the temple courts. They broke bread in their homes and ate together with glad and sincere hearts" (Acts 2:42–46).

These early believers expected the Lord to return imminently, and they saw all the work that they did during the week as well as on the Sabbath as work for the Lord, for His Church. Their joy was in the Lord and in His plan. They were excited about Jesus the Messiah. They knew Him intimately. But by the time the Lord judged the church at Ephesus, about sixty years later, a second generation had lost this excitement. They were working hard to build His church, but their focus was on the works they were doing and not on the Lord. Jesus said to them, "You have forsaken your first love" (Rev. 2:4). They were like the believers in the church at Laodicea whom Jesus said were "neither cold nor hot" (Rev. 3:15).

When John heard the indictment against the believers at Ephesus, it must have pierced his heart. Jesus was the center of John's life. The glow of that first love he had for the Son of God never left him. On the Isle of Patmos, he must have spent his time worshiping, talking, and listening to God. He wrote down the words that God said to him, pondered them, lived by them. The believers at Ephesus, however, had lost their excitement of loving and serving Jesus. It happened when they changed their focus and their zeal cooled.

In his book *Storm Warning*, Billy Graham has this to say about the problem: "Christ was calling the Ephesians and the Laodiceans away from respectable, comfortable, passionless, lukewarm religion. He wanted them totally committed to Him, wholeheartedly available. He called them back to the holy passion and the joy of their first love. They had settled instead for mere theological respectability and material comfort. He wanted them alive, depending, risking, passionate again."[1]

Think back to the time you first came to know Jesus, the time you were so filled with His love that you could think of little else. If you were like me, you wanted to spend time with Jesus in prayer and in His Word every day. You wanted to be with other believers to talk about Jesus. You wanted to tell everyone you knew about your wonderful Lord. If you still share this intimacy with Jesus day by day, then you are indeed blessed. If you are like many other Christians, there are days when you feel overburdened with work—even work for His Church—and you struggle to return to "your first love."

The Solution

Jesus had the solution to the problem which He found in the church at Ephesus. What He had to say to those believers is good advice for us. "Remember the height from which you have fallen! Repent and do the things you did at first. . . . To him who overcomes, I will give the right to eat from the tree of life, which is in the paradise of God" (Rev. 2:5a, 7b).

Remember. Repent. Return. That's the key if we want to be restored to the joy we once knew. Let's consider these commands of Jesus one at a time that we may learn how to correct our problem when the Spirit reminds us that our focus is on our works and calls us to return to "our first love."

Remember

Contrary to what many people believe today, we do learn from the past. We learn both from the successes and the failures of those who have gone before us. That's part of God's plan. The Old Testament in particular is filled with the history of God's people as they lived their lives day by day. Sometimes they walked in God's plan and were richly blessed. Other times they chose to go their own way and experienced frustration and separation from God. God expects us to learn from these recorded lessons.

In the Old Testament, the word *remember* is used 130 times. Let's take a look at a few of the things God wanted His people to remember. As you read, apply them to your own life. They are as relevant today as they were in centuries past.

- "Remember the everlasting covenant" (Gen. 9:16).
  Do you believe that God will always keep His promises?
- "Remember the Sabbath" (Exod. 20:8).
  How do you spend the Sabbath?
- "Remember to obey all my commands" (Num. 15:40).
  Are you obeying God in all things?
- "Remember that you were slaves in Egypt and the LORD your God redeemed you" (Deut. 15:15).
  Do you often praise God for saving you from slavery to sin and giving you eternal life?
- "Remember how the LORD your God led you all the way in the desert these forty years" (Deut. 8:2).
  Has God not led you through dry times before?
- "Remember the days of old; consider the generations long past" (Deut. 32:7).
  Hasn't God always been faithful—generation to generation?
- "Remember the wonders he has done, his miracles, and the judgments he pronounced" (1 Chron. 16:12).
  Name them. Are you encouraged?
- "Remember the LORD who is great and awesome" (Neh. 4:14).
  When you come before God, are you remembering His majesty, His holiness?

- "Remember to extol his work, which men have praised in song" (Job 36:24).
  Pause and praise Him!

The New Testament also calls us to remember. Jesus was deeply concerned that His disciples remember all that He taught them by word and by example. "'Do you have eyes but fail to see, and ears but fail to hear? And don't you remember?'" He asked them (Mark 8:18). Later, Jesus warned them, "'Remember the words I spoke to you'" (John 15:20).

Like Jesus, Paul wanted his teaching to be remembered. He wrote to Timothy, "Remember Jesus Christ, raised from the dead, descended from David. This is my gospel" (2 Tim. 2:8). Paul's words to the church at Ephesus are especially relevant to us today. Paul called them to look back on their lives. "Remember that at that time you were separate from Christ, excluded from citizenship in Israel and foreigners to the covenants of the promise, without hope and without God in the world" (Eph. 2:12).

Do you ever think what your life would have been like had you never come to know Jesus as Savior and Lord? I do. It helps to remember. But we are to go forward and "remember those earlier days after you had received the light" (Heb. 10:32). I like to remember those who taught me about Jesus—my parents, Sunday school teachers, pastors, and friends. I have a dear friend who taught me to work hard in school because that was pleasing to the Lord, and she taught me by her example to care for the needs of others. Miss Ada Margaret Smith was my fourth grade teacher, and we still keep in touch because I remember.

Remembering causes us to renew our vision of God's plan which is eternal, everlasting, never failing. We remember what God has done for His people throughout the ages. We remember what He has done for us, the miracles that He has brought about in our lives. Our eyes and hearts are then focused on our awesome God. Like King

David when he had wandered so far away from God's plan for his life, we cry out to God, "Restore to me the joy of your salvation and grant me a willing spirit, to sustain me" (Ps. 51:12).

Repent

What can cause us to lose our first love? Why do we need to repent? The answer could be many things. Let's examine two carefully.

First, we may have fallen into the trap of thinking that only the work we do on Sundays or in direct relationship to some church program can be considered "ministry." Not so. Jesus ministered in the world far more than He ministered in the synagogue. The evangelical mission of the Church is to equip believers and send them out to do the work of ministry. While some are called to the primary ministry of equipping believers, far more are called to working daily among unbelievers. The Lord places us wherever there is a need, and we may be the only believers in our office, our store, our schoolroom, and our home. If so, our primary ministry may be to teach there by example, by sharing what we have learned within the church body. That is our mission field. And it is important work. If then we are so overburdened with "church work" that we neglect the ministry Christ has chosen for us, we need to repent.

Let me give you some examples of people I know whose primary ministry is sharing the love of Jesus daily in the workplace. At one time some of them began to feel overburdened with committees, programs, and offices where they had agreed to serve, and their ministries were no longer joyful experiences. Now they are working within a broader vision of God's plan.

Beth, who is in my Thursday night care group, teaches at the college nearby. That campus is her mission field. Everyone knows she is a Christian, and students often come to her with their problems. Beth has the answer. She prays for her students, shares her faith in Christ Jesus, and ministers to them in many ways.

Another member of our group teaches in elementary school. Alice has a deep love for her students. As she teaches them the basic skills, she prays that God will open doors for her to share God's answer to the important questions of life. Alice has a special ministry within God's plan.

Tom, Domingo, and Jim travel all over the United States and are always open to opportunities to share their faith—on the plane, in the office, with strangers, and with fellow workers. At home, Tom's wife Jan focuses her ministry at this time on her family. Her mother is in a convalescent care center and needs Jan's love, encouragement, and care. Since her mother is fifty miles away, Jan must make frequent trips between Lompoc and Santa Barbara. This is Jan's work, her ministry, and it's important.

My husband, Al, has the gift of helping others. He goes into the homes of believers and unbelievers fixing broken light switches, repairing appliances, and caring for the sick. In his workshop he makes stained-glass windows to brighten the homes of those who need a little cheer. He is sensitive to the needs of others, prays for and with them, and has great joy in meeting their needs. Al is serving the Lord with the special gift the Spirit has given him, and God's love shines through him.

Turning back to the plan Jesus has for our lives can relieve the tension we feel when we are overloaded and overburdened with good works. "Repent," Jesus said, "and do the things you did at first." When we have lost the joy of our first love, Jesus' words are for us. Repent and return.

Second, we may have lost our first love because we took on ministries which the Lord may well have intended for others. In many churches a few people do most of the work. Yet God's Word teaches us that every believer has gifts for ministry. We are all parts of one body. The "eye cannot say to the hand, 'I don't need you!'" At the same time, the eye and the hand have different functions. This must mean that we should prayerfully choose to minister in areas where God has equipped and placed us.

Highly efficient people often discourage us from entering the very ministries to which God is calling us. "No one can organize a dinner like Peggy," we say, or, "I could never learn to comfort the sick like Gary." We need efficient people to teach us, train us, and allow us to work beside them in ministry. My friend Helen is like this. She is a wedding coordinator. She plans everything in detail and brings the occasion together in perfect harmony. Best of all, Helen allows others to help her—and we all enjoy the fellowship, the joy of working together. This is Helen's only ministry within the church even though we all know she could do many more things very well! But she ministers during the week to her family, her friends, her coworkers. And she guards her time with the Lord.

Catherine has limited her ministry to assisting our care group leader. Thoughtful and caring, she organizes our group for shared dinners, drops "reminder" cards before each meeting, and calls us when someone needs help. Carol and Tony disciple young couples and move them into ministry. Gary is an encourager who reminds us by word and by example just as Paul reminded the Colossians, "It is the Lord Christ you are serving" (3:24).

How easy it is to overload ourselves with tasks which become burdens rather than joys and which take works of ministries away from others who need to be involved. Is it our pride which takes over? Is it our belief that we are the only ones who can do the work of ministry? Or do we believe that the more work we do the better Christians we are? If we neglect our time with Jesus, fail to spend time with Him in prayer and in His Word, if we are just too busy to hear His voice, then it is time to repent and return to our first love. It was Jesus who said, "'My yoke is easy and my burden is light'" (Matt. 11:30).

Return

The prophets Isaiah and Jeremiah remind us that God will forgive us, help us, and care for us. Isaiah wrote, "You come to the help of those who gladly do right, who remember your ways" (64:5). And Jeremiah said, "You understand, O LORD; remember me and care for me" (15:15).

God will restore to us the joy of our salvation when we repent and return to our "first love," Jesus, as our focus. But, how can we begin again? We begin by setting aside a special time each day to *be* with Jesus. Of course, we know that He is always with us, but in our busy lives we need a quiet time when we can focus on our first love and listen. Spending time in the Word will help us to find the particular work the Lord wants us to do. Every believer has a place in His plan.

A number of years ago we started a plan in our church to help every believer find a ministry. We began by focusing on equipping believers to serve in ministries related to their spiritual gifts. We prayed diligently that God would open doors to ministries that would help fulfill His plan. He did. Each believer was equipped to take a major ministry and a minor ministry—no more. A major ministry was one which would take time, effort, and work. The believer was often the one directly responsible for this ministry. It might be teaching a Sunday school class, counseling, working with the food pantry or thrift shop downtown, or singing in the choir. A minor ministry was one which occurred occasionally: helping others with their ministries now and then, planning a luncheon, providing hospitality for a visiting missionary speaker, or collecting food baskets at Christmastime.

We all became excited about the many opportunities all about us. Many ministries which were formerly handled by only a few now became available for others. An added bonus was the joy and relief which all of us enjoyed by being able to say, "No, I can't take that on now. I have both a major and a minor ministry, and God's blessing me!"

We also discovered that not all ministries are meant to last forever. God knows the needs about us, and these can be either short-term or long-term needs. We were never afraid to say, "We no longer need this ministry." At other times, we were guilty of pushing ahead of the Spirit's guidance, and the ministry failed. Then we backed up and started over.

We strongly encouraged everyone serving in a major ministry to train another person in that ministry. Paul trained Timothy. Barnabas trained John Mark. In our church, this plan of sharing ministry developed many loving relationships. It also provided relief and often rest for the person responsible for the ministry.

You may be wondering if Ann ever regained her excitement about serving Jesus. Indeed she did. She turned over her Sunday school class to the assistant she had been training for months. She resigned from the choir, resigned from leadership in Women's Association and Prison Fellowship. Then she took the summer off to get reacquainted with Jesus. In the fall, she returned with a new excitement, a new passion for ministry. "I'll never again get so busy that I don't have time for Jesus," Ann told her new class of adults. "If I can't spend time with Him, I'll have nothing to give you." That's the lesson. That's returning to your first love.

Discovering His Plans

1. Make a list of all the things you do each week which you consider "ministry." Now check those items which

you believe are in the area of your spiritual gifts. What did you learn?

2. Consider the list you made. What three things on your list brought you the most satisfaction? Which things were a burden?

3. How much time did you spend this week in prayer? In study of God's Word? Did your list of ministries keep you from your special time with the Lord? In what way does your time spent with the Lord affect your ministry?

4. Do you feel satisfied that you are following God's plan in (a) giving Him top priority in your life, and in (b) serving Him in ministries to which He has called you?

5. If your answers to the last question were no, ask God to help you work through the steps of (a) remember, (b) repent, and (c) return.

12

Called to Suffer

I first met Bob Cleath at an InterVarsity Christian Fellowship weekend retreat in Watsonville, California, several years ago. He was a professor in the speech department at Cal Poly University. I learned from Bob much of what it means to suffer as a Christian because he bore in his face the marks of intense suffering.

The Cleaths were preparing for Christmas with their four children when they received news that their son, Rob, was severely injured in a car accident. He was on his way home from Wheaton College in Illinois. For the next thirteen years Virginia and Bob Cleath visited their son daily in the rest home where he lay in a coma. He never regained consciousness. The Cleath family was a shining example of following Jesus through suffering, dying inside, and rising in His strength. Observing their response to suffering affected the lives of hundreds of students.

This past summer the son of close friends of ours was on a retreat with some high school students and fell from a high cliff. When the rescue squad reached him, he was dead. Two doors down the street from me, Marie, a beautiful Christian lady and a member of our care group, died of cancer. A year before her own death, Marie lost her husband to the same illness.

Our nation has suffered through floods, earthquakes, and riots. The tragedy resulting from the bombing of the Federal Building in Oklahoma City left hundreds of families in deep mourning. These were innocent people. Why did they have to suffer?

In Japan, suffering and death came to hundreds of people from the senseless release of poisonous gasses by cult members. Around the world, plane crashes, war, terror, and torture are daily occurrences. The pain comes to people of all races and creeds and circumstances. Why?

As Christians, we might expect that we would suffer less than nonbelievers or that by this century we would have been able to reduce suffering in the world. However, not one of us will escape the pain which comes with the death of a loved one—not if we live long enough. Most of us at some time in life will know the pain of serious illness, separation, or divorce. Of unexpected violence. Of bigotry, criticism, or some other tragedy common to life. Around the globe Christians still give up their lives for the sake of Jesus Christ. According to Christian Solidarity International, "More Christians have been murdered for their faith in the 20th century than all other centuries combined. It is believed that more than 150,000 Christians are martyred every year and nearly two-thirds of the world's population live in countries where Christians are persecuted."[1]

We can't escape these dark and lonely valleys. And we don't always know why we suffer, but it is God's plan that we be victorious.

We Can't Avoid the Valleys

Believers sometimes make the mistake of painting a trouble-free picture of the Christian life for unbelievers.

Perhaps we do this because we think it will encourage unbelievers to come into God's kingdom. Yet nowhere in the Bible are we told to expect good health or wealth or lives free of pain and sorrow when we choose to follow Jesus. Instead, Jesus said, "'If anyone would come after me, he must deny himself and take up his cross and follow me'" (Mark 8:34). That does not sound like an easy path. Jesus' life was hard. He didn't have many earthly possessions. He didn't own a house, have many clothes, or even have a donkey. He wasn't interested in being king of Judea or head of the Sanhedrin. During the three years of His ministry, He was persecuted, rejected, ridiculed, and finally put to death on the cross. Jesus suffered. No, when we choose to follow Jesus, we do not choose an easy path.

Peter, the big fisherman, was close to the heart of Jesus. Yet it was not until he saw Jesus rise victoriously above His suffering that Peter understood what it meant to "deny himself, take up his cross, and follow" Jesus. Only then was Peter able to write, "To this you were called, because Christ suffered for you, leaving you an example, that you should follow in his steps" (1 Pet. 2:21).

Peter did suffer for the cause of Christ. He was put in prison, beaten, rejected by both Jews and Gentiles. While there are no records before A.D. 170 to show that Peter was ever in Rome, some claim that he died there, martyred by Nero in A.D. 64. Tradition says that Peter requested that he be crucified with his head to the ground as he did not consider himself worthy to die as Jesus died.

Kendrick Strong, in his book *All the Master's Men,* gives us insight into the severe persecution suffered by all of Jesus' disciples. He shares some of the ancient traditions surrounding their deaths. One account states that Andrew was tied to a cross where he hung for three days before he died. During that time, he continued to tell all those who stood at the foot of his cross about Jesus. Nathanael is said to have been martyred in Armenia. Eusebius, an early writer, wrote that Philip was put to death in Hierapolis.² We are told in Acts 12:2 that James, the brother of John, was killed by the sword by order of Herod Agrippa in A.D. 44. As far as we know, the only disciple not to die by violent means was John, who suffered many years in exile on the Isle of Patmos.

These men lived with Jesus during His earthly ministry. They lived obedient, Spirit-filled lives after the resurrection, spreading the gospel message throughout the known world. Yet they knew the meaning of pain and sorrow. Since the disciples did not escape trials, should we expect to go free? No, we too must follow Jesus.

Pain is on our path. It intrudes on our lives. And there is no escape. We must go through the valleys if we want to reach the top of the mountain.

We Question the Justice of Suffering

In the Old Testament book by his name, Job could not understand why he had lost everything that he loved. First, the Sabeans attacked, carrying off his oxen and donkeys, and killing his servants. Next, lightning struck his sheep, and only one sheepherder escaped. Then, the Chaldeans carried off his camels. Last, a tornado struck his oldest son's house where Job's family was feasting. When the house collapsed, all Job's sons and daughters were killed.

How could Job understand the loss of everything he loved? He couldn't. He knew he was a righteous man. And he knew God was just. Yet suffering had come upon him and he had no explanation. "'I cry out to you, O God,'" Job said, "'but you do not answer; I stand up, but you merely look at me. . . . When I looked for good, evil came; when I looked for light, then came darkness'" (Job 30:20, 26).

Have you ever felt like Job? Sometimes we know we are faithful to God. We center our lives in the church. We serve other people. We pray, read our Bibles, love everyone. Yet trouble comes. "Why? Why me?" we ask.

Job's friends insisted that Job's troubles came because he had sinned. The Israelites believed at that time that God punished sin by bringing suffering upon the sinner. Job's friends pleaded with him to repent, to ask God's forgiveness. "'Hardship does not spring from the soil, nor does trouble sprout from the ground,'" Eliphaz said (Job 5:6). Zophar was quick to advise Job: "'If you put away the sin that is in your hand and allow no evil to dwell in your tent, then you will lift up your face without shame; . . . You will surely forget your trouble'" (Job 11:14–16).

Job could not accept the argument of his friends that suffering comes as a punishment from God. Instead, he cried out to God for an answer to his pain, and God answered by asking Job, "'Who is this that darkens my counsel with words without knowledge?'" Then He said, "'Brace yourself like a man; I will question you and you shall answer me'" (Job 38:2–3). And God did question Job, causing His servant to realize His mighty power, sovereignty, and holiness. Look at some of God's questions:

"Where were you when I laid the earth's foundation?"
   (38:4)

"Who shut up the sea behind doors
   when it burst forth from the womb?" (38:8)

"Have you ever given orders to the morning,
   or shown the dawn its place
that it might take the earth by the edges
   and shake the wicked out of it?" (38:12)

"Who endowed the heart with wisdom
   or gave understanding to the mind?" (38:36)

"Do you give the horse his strength
   or clothe his neck with a flowing mane?" (39:19)

"Does the eagle soar at your command
  and build his nest on high?" (39:27)

God revealed Himself to Job through many questions.
Then He asked: "'Will the one who contends with the
Almighty correct him? Let him who accuses God answer
him!'" (40:2).

Then Job answered the Lord: "'You asked, "Who is this
that obscures my counsel without knowledge?" Surely I
spoke of things I did not understand, . . . Therefore I
despise myself and repent in dust and ashes'" (42:3, 6).

In the beginning, God created a world without pain. A
world free from suffering. Free from sin. But through the
disobedience of Adam and Eve, sin entered the world.
God in His absolute justice pronounced a sentence of
death. Dr. Billy Graham explains this three-dimensional
death as: "(1) Instant spiritual death: separation from God.
(2) Gradual physical death: as soon as we are born we
begin to die. (3) Ultimate eternal death—but for the saving mercy of Jesus Christ."[3]

The battle against sin and suffering began in the garden
of Eden, and it is part of our world and our lives today.
"Just as sin entered the world through one man, and death
through sin," Paul wrote, "in this way death came to all
men, because all sinned" (Rom. 5:12). We cannot blame
God for our suffering, but we do know that He has a plan
to turn our suffering into good. He has the power to turn
every moment of our pain into victory for His kingdom.

We Can Be Victorious over Suffering

Our God is still a God of miracles. He often heals the
sick and miraculously touches the brokenhearted when we
ask. But the experience that Paul had with suffering helps
us to understand that God does not always change our circumstances when we cry out to Him in our pain—not
always. In his letter to the Corinthian Christians, Paul

spoke about a thorn in his flesh, "a messenger of Satan," that tormented him. We aren't sure what this was, but it must have been painful. Three times Paul asked God to take away this suffering, but each time God said, "My grace is sufficient for you, for my power is made perfect in weakness" (2 Cor. 12:9). Paul recognized that because he had a position of authority and leadership in the building of the Church, he could easily become arrogant and boastful. God's plan was to keep Paul humble and dependent upon Him. "That is why, for Christ's sake, I delight in weaknesses," Paul said, "in insults, in hardships, in persecutions, in difficulties. For when I am weak, then I am strong" (2 Cor. 12:10). Paul valued God's plan for his life, God's peace and comfort, far more than being relieved of personal suffering. He rose above his circumstances, and he grew in God's grace.

Allow God to Teach

Like Paul, we can choose to allow God to teach us, to strengthen us, and to give us the power to grow stronger in Him through our suffering. James wrote, "Consider it pure joy, my brothers, whenever you face trials of many kinds, because you know that the testing of your faith develops perseverance" (James 1:2). The apostle Peter's words can also encourage us: "If you are suffering according to God's will, keep on doing what is right and trust yourself to the God who made you, for he will never fail you" (1 Pet. 4:19, TLB).

We have a choice. We can trust God who has promised that He will never leave us. We can trust His plan for our lives. We can trust His grace to comfort, strengthen, and bring us through our trials. When my sister lost her husband to cancer two years ago, she made this choice. She chose to trust God and move forward in His plan for her life. "I chose to get out of the house every day at least for a short time," Rita said, "and to get involved with people."

She is a worker in her church and a volunteer at the Salvation Army thrift store. She is available to her family, friends, and anyone else who needs her help. She can say with David, "The Lord is my strength and my shield; my heart trusts in Him, and I am helped" (Ps. 28:7).

The alternative choice is to reject God's love and grace when trouble strikes. Some people do. They blame God for their troubles. They either struggle to overcome suffering in their own strength or they retreat from life into a well of sorrow. God has numbered our days. Is He pleased when we waste them in this way?

Reflect God's Grace

When God does not take us out of our suffering, He wants our lives to be a reflection of His grace. We may be used of God to fulfill His plan in someone else's life. Are we willing to suffer for Christ's sake? To suffer that others may know God's love and saving grace? Many believers are, but it takes God's power within us to hold us. When we are in Christ Jesus and His Spirit is within us, we can live in His power, His strength, and His grace. He is greater than our suffering and our pain.

In their book *In His Image*, Dr. Paul Brand and Philip Yancey explain, "The pictorial Chinese language combines the two concepts of love and pain in eloquent symbolism. In the character that expresses the highest kind of love, symbols for love and for pain are brushed on top of each other to form a word like 'pain-love.' Thus, a mother 'pain-loves' her child. She pours out her whole being on the child's behalf."[4]

God's grace is like that. On the cross, the love of Jesus for us covered His pain and suffering. We know the meaning of His "pain-love" today when He takes His brush and paints over our pain with His love.

Our family experienced this truth. When I was twelve years old, the doctors discovered that my mother had a brain tumor. She was thirty-seven years of age and president of the Women's Missionary Society in our church. Dad was a deacon, a high-school Sunday school teacher, and both my parents were committed to serving Jesus Christ. When mother became ill, Dad had no hospitalization insurance. He mortgaged everything we had and borrowed money for mother's hospital expenses at Baylor Hospital in Dallas, Texas.

After three operations and six months of round-the-clock nursing care in the hospital, Dad brought Mother home. She was blind and had limited speech. Her memory and thought processes were not harmed by the tumor, and we were grateful to God who spared her life when doctors told us there was little chance of survival.

Through the years I watched the loving care my dad gave Mother and our family, and I watched the courage and faith of a mother who trusted the Lord in all circumstances. Their lives were a reflection of God's grace and strength. God used their patient suffering as an influence not only on our family but on all who knew them.

When Dad died of a heart attack in 1979, my two sisters and I rushed home to be with Mother, feeling that she would be desperate with Dad gone; however, she strengthened us and all of her grandchildren who came from across the United States to be with her. She was eighty years old and lived only a year after Dad died, but that year was a year of victory. She was a tower of strength and joy, a constant reminder that Jesus is Lord of all—even of our pain and suffering.

Trust and Do Not Fear

I love the words of the Lord found in Isaiah 4:1–3.

"Fear not, for I have redeemed you;
    I have summoned you by name; you are mine.
When you pass through the waters,
    I will be with you;

156

and when you pass through the rivers,
   they will not sweep over you.

When you walk through the fire,
   you will not be burned;
   the flames will not set you ablaze.
For I am the LORD, your God,
   the Holy One of Israel, your Savior."

Amy Carmichael spent fifty-six years in India as a missionary without a furlough. She was bedridden the last twenty years of her life as a result of a fall. During this time she wrote many books about serving Jesus, thirteen of them while enduring severe pain. On her wall hung four words from Revelation 2:9–10: "I know . . . fear not."

As believers in a loving God who provides us with everything we need, we must learn to trust His plan and His promise to be with us. In her book, *Goodbye Is Not Forever*, Amy George tells of her family's severe suffering under the Communists in Russia and later under the Nazis in Germany during World War II. Then she closes the story with these words:

> I now recognize that God was there all the time, even when I and my family were not aware of a living God. He saw us through all our troubles. . . . He kept my family from starving during the years of famine in Russia. . . . He kept us safe from bombs and artillery attacks when the Germans invaded our land. . . . He kept us alive as we worked and endured the harsh conditions in the labor camp in Nazi Germany. . . . During times when death was commonplace, He kept every member of our family alive. He then chose to reveal His Son to each of us, one by one. Yes . . . He guided our lives. Why? Because He had a plan—an eternal plan that none of us knew.[5]

Like Amy George's family, Dietrich Bonhoeffer suffered exile, prison, and torment in the 1940s. His suffering came because of his outspoken faith in Jesus Christ. Yet he never wavered in his testimony that the grace of God was sufficient. "After he has been following Christ for a long time," Bonhoeffer wrote, "the disciple of Jesus will be asked, 'Lacked ye anything?' and he will answer 'Nothing, Lord.' How could he when he knows that despite hunger and nakedness, persecution and danger, the Lord is always at his side?"[6]

When trouble comes, we must be ready to say, "Lord, I don't have to know why. I just have to know how you want me to respond to this pain. I know you have a plan for my life and will give me your peace and your grace."

Discovering His Plans

1. What evidence can you give that "we can't avoid the valleys"? Why do you think this is true?

2. How can we be victorious over suffering?

3. What are some of the lessons God teaches us when we go through suffering?

4. In what ways can we reflect God's grace when we suffer? Give examples.

5. Memorize Isaiah 43:1–3. How can these verses help you to trust God's plan for the world and for your life?

13

Called to Forgive

I never knew Uncle Willie, but few people in my family tree have had a greater influence on the generations that separate us. As a child when I asked why some of my cousins went to church and others didn't, Uncle Willie was always the focus of the explanation. He lived in the days when Texas was fast developing a ranching industry and herds of cattle were driven to California. Uncle Willie lived on the trails. He was a renegade—from the family, from society, and from God. When he was killed in a gunfight, and his body returned for burial, the family gathered around.

Fearing that the pastor would have a hard time finding good things to say about his brother at the funeral, Uncle Jonathan made him a list. At the top of the page he wrote "Willie's good deeds to be read at his funeral." The pastor was disturbed. What was he to do? He prayed. He struggled. And he made the decision to ignore the list. In the service, he said nothing good about Uncle Willie. I've been told his words were not very comforting.

On his way out the door at the close of the service, Uncle Jonathan said to the good pastor, "You're not needed at the cemetery, Pastor. I'll bury my brother. And I assure you, our family will never enter the doors of this church again!"

However, he didn't speak for the third brother, my great-grandfather. I'll always be grateful for the decision he made that day. "My family and I will never leave our God or His church," he said. The family divided. Half left the church, never to return. Half stayed in the church. The results of one brother's choice not to forgive and the other brother's choice to forgive are still seen in the division of my family line today.

Unforgiveness can raise its ugly head at any point in our Christian walk. It can change our lives and the lives of generations after us. It is a serious sin. Yet in today's world we are too prone to agree with the sign on the bulletin board of a large manufacturing company which reads: "To err is human; to forgive is not company policy."

Forgiveness is the policy of our Lord Jesus Christ. It's part of His plan. He taught by word and by example that if we are to be His disciples, members of His family, we must forgive. Richard Strauss wrote, "A person who has honestly admitted to the vileness of his own sin, and has experienced the blessing of God's forgiveness, cannot help but respond with forgiveness toward others." Deep in our hearts we know this is true, but forgiveness does not always come without a struggle.

Answering three basic questions should help us deal with this struggle: (1) Why should we forgive? (2) Who should we forgive? (3) How should we forgive?

Why Should We Forgive?

Unforgiveness Is Harmful

From a purely selfish viewpoint, we should forgive to preserve our health. Statistics show that more than half of illnesses in general hospitals are thought to stem from the roots of bitterness, hatred, and resentment—all fruits of unforgiveness. This sin can manifest itself in ulcers, headaches, paralysis, and various forms of mental illnesses.

We've all known people who refused to forgive friends, children, parents, and so missed the joy of close relationships while suffering from bitterness in their hearts. We wonder why they choose to punish themselves so harshly. This is sin.

When I was growing up, an elderly lady lived alone in a house across the highway from our place. Mrs. Dobish seldom went out of the house. When she did, she walked with her head down, stumbling along and leaning on a cane. Her dresses were always to her ankles and often her shoe laces were untied. I seldom saw her face because she wore a bonnet tied under the chin, but I knew some things about Mrs. Dobish. I knew she had a son whom she had banished from her presence. It happened when he married a girl from a family his mother disliked. He never came to visit; no one did. Not for more than fifty years. When Mrs. Dobish died, no one knew. She died alone in her home. The police discovered her body when Dad called them to check on her because we hadn't seen her trudging down the road to the grocer in over a week. A choice not to forgive can have bitter results.

I once heard a reporter ask the mother of a young girl who had been assaulted if she could ever forgive the man who injured her child. The woman replied, "In time we'll get on with our lives and try to forget, but never, never will I forgive him!"

Jesus must have met many people like this, but holding on to hurt and anger and vindictiveness was not His way.

Jesus Is Our Example

As we follow Jesus through the pages of the Four Gospels, we see Him forgiving people again and again. One

The Plans of His Heart

day Jesus saw Matthew, a tax collector who worked for the Roman government, and called him to be His disciple. That was a big step. Like all tax collectors of his day, Matthew probably had a goal: collect all the taxes you can and keep for yourself as much as possible. I doubt if Matthew had much compassion or honesty or desire to change his ways—until he met Jesus. The religious people of Matthew's day called him a publican, a sinner. Never would they go to his house for a meal or socialize with him in any way. Jesus did. He saw not what this tax collector was, but what he could become. Matthew's life was changed, totally changed, because Jesus forgave him (Matt. 9:9–12).

Jesus even forgave Peter when he denied knowing Him—three times. He forgave the other disciples who failed to stand by Him when He needed them the most. The hardest for me would have been to forgive those Pharisees and scribes who plotted against Him. They harassed Jesus during His ministry. They were responsible for His arrest and His crucifixion. But Jesus said, "'Love your enemies and pray for those who persecute you'" (Matt. 5:44). That's what He did. As He hung on the cross, Jesus prayed for those who beat Him and laughed at Him and drove the nails into His flesh. That's hard. But that's forgiveness.

Paul is a good example of the gracious forgiveness of Jesus. His Hebrew name was Saul. We know him by that name at the time he persecuted Christians and killed them. He even stood by and watched the crowd stone Stephen, a devout follower of Jesus. Saul didn't have much compassion then. He wasn't at all like Jesus. When Jesus met Saul on the road to Damascus, He forgave him. Then He called him to become Paul the apostle, missionary to the Gentiles, and writer of at least half of the books in our New Testament.

Are we forgiven any less than Matthew? Peter? Paul? No, we've all rejected Jesus at some time in our lives, said no when He called us to come and obey. John wrote, "If we confess our sins, he is faithful and just and will forgive us our sins, . . ." and, "Your sins have been forgiven on account of his name" (1 John 1:9; 2:12).

Jesus paid the price for all our sins when He died on Calvary's cross. This was God's plan to save us. "I tell you the truth," He said, "whoever hears my word and believes him who sent me has eternal life and will not be condemned; he has crossed over from death to life" (John 5:24). Yes, that's forgiveness. Great joy wells up within us when we know that Jesus has forgiven our sins and received us into His family.

The story Jesus told of the prodigal son has always been a comfort to me. You'll find it in Luke 15:11–32. A man had two sons. At the younger son's request, the father divided between his sons their share of his estate. A few days later the younger son left his home and, by loose living, squandered all that he had been given. When everything was gone, he returned to his father saying, "'Father, I have sinned against heaven and against you. I am no longer worthy to be called your son; make me like one of your hired men.'" His father was loving and compassionate. He embraced his son and ordered his slaves to bring a robe, a ring for his finger, and sandals for his feet. Then he planned a great feast to celebrate the return of his son. That's how God forgives us and receives us when we wander from the path He's chosen for us. He loves us unconditionally.

How, then, can we fail to forgive others when Jesus has forgiven us? Paul's plea to the Colossians is just as relevant for us: "Bear with each other and forgive whatever grievances you may have against one another. Forgive as the Lord forgave you" (3:13). He's our example. We are to forgive like Jesus.

Jesus Commanded Forgiveness

Jesus said, "'When you stand praying, if you hold anything against anyone, forgive him, so that your Father in heaven may forgive you your sins'" (Mark 11:25). Only after we have forgiven others can we pray, "Forgive us our debts, as we also have forgiven our debtors" (Matt. 6:12). So serious is the sin of unforgiveness that Jesus issued a warning. "'If you forgive men when they sin against you,'" He said, "'your heavenly Father will also forgive you. But if you do not forgive men their sins, your Father will not forgive your sins'" (Matt. 6:14–15).

Jesus illustrated this teaching with a parable found in Matthew 18:23–35. Once, Jesus said, a servant owed the king ten thousand talents but was unable to pay. When the king ordered that the man's family and all that he owned be sold to pay his debt, the man pleaded for mercy. The king took pity on him, canceled his debt, and set him free.

The man went out and found one of his fellow servants who owed him a hundred denarii. He grabbed him and demanded that the servant pay him what he owed. The servant fell to his knees and begged, "Be patient with me, and I will pay you back." The man refused and had his fellow servant thrown in prison.

When the king heard what had happened, he called his wicked servant to him and asked, "Shouldn't you have had mercy on your fellow servant just as I had on you?" When the servant could give no answer, the king turned him over to the jailers.

I don't want to be like the unforgiving servant. I want to be a reflection of Jesus. Don't you? He has given us an example to follow. He has commanded us to forgive. When He has so lovingly forgiven us, how can we refuse to obey Him and to forgive others? We can't.

Whom Should We Forgive?

Ourselves

Forgiving ourselves is not always easy. Several years ago a dedicated air force chaplain arrived in Greenland to begin a tour of duty. One morning he was late for work and backed his car out of the garage without checking for a buildup of snow as he usually did, but this morning more than snow was in the driveway. The next door neighbor's three-year-old child had wandered outside to play and was unaware of the approaching danger. The impact of the chaplain's car killed the little boy instantly.

For weeks the chaplain was unable to minister to himself or to others. "If only I had looked before backing out," he said. "If only I had not been in a hurry. If, if, if . . . ." One day the little boy's parents walked across the yard and knocked on the chaplain's door. "Their warmth and for-giveness touched something deep inside me," the chaplain said later. "As my neighbor led us in prayer, I was able to share my pain with God and know His loving forgiveness. Only then was I able to forgive myself."

When I was on church staff, I spent many hours with a young girl who had an abortion when she was a senior in high school. She was now married and had two children, but even after ten years, she could not forget the one she had lost. "I murdered my own child!" she said over and over again as she sobbed through her pain. I listened and cried with Jane, but my words gave her little comfort. Only after much prayer and encouragement was she able to realize that God had forgiven her and that she must forgive herself.

Some people think they have committed the unforgive-able sin which Jesus talks about in Mark 3:28–29. Since they believe God will not forgive them, they cannot for-give themselves. Jesus said: "'I tell you the truth, all the sins and blasphemies of men will be forgiven them. But whoever blasphemes against the Holy Spirit will never be forgiven; he is guilty of an eternal sin.'"

I once visited an elderly man in the hospital who said to me, "I have a great fear of dying because I have committed the unforgivable sin. For years I used the Lord's name in vain—blasphemy again and again. He'll never forgive me for that even though I've tried for years to do right. And even if God forgave me, I could never forgive myself—not after all I've said against Him." I remembered when John had started attending our church. And I knew he had a kind and gentle heart. He was always willing to drive disabled people to the doctor or teenagers to camp. John never said no. That's why I was surprised when he shared his fear. I reached for my Bible and turned to Mark 3:20–29.

Like John, many people fail to understand what Jesus said about this unforgivable sin. Jesus was dealing with the teachers of the law who attributed the miracles He performed to Satan. "'He is possessed by Beelzebub!'" they said. "'By the prince of demons he is driving out demons.'" Jesus said they were wrong. "'In fact,'" He said, "'no one can enter a strong man's house and carry off his possessions unless he first ties up the strong man.'" Then Jesus said to them, "'Whoever blasphemes against the Holy Spirit will never be forgiven; he is guilty of an eternal sin.'"

The unforgivable sin Jesus warned the teachers of the Law about was the sin of rejecting the truth, and His words stand as a warning today. Continued rejection of the Holy Spirit's calling brings hardness of heart. We are taught this truth even in the Old Testament. Remember Pharaoh? Note the progression in the Exodus story: "Pharaoh's heart became hard" (7:13). "When Pharaoh saw that there was relief, he hardened his heart" (8:15). "Pharaoh's heart was hard" (8:19). "Pharaoh hardened his heart" (8:32). "Yet his heart was unyielding" (9:7). "But the LORD hardened Pharaoh's heart" (9:12).

Since Jesus Christ is our only Savior and the only way to God and eternal life, rejecting Him again and again does indeed cause hearts to become harder and harder. In time these hearts no longer hear. Then there is danger of dying with the sin which cannot be forgiven.

When I closed my Bible, John's eyes were filled with tears. "Do you mean I've lived all these years believing I couldn't be forgiven?" he asked.

"I suspect God forgave you long ago," I said. "But let's pray together and you share with Jesus what is on your heart."

This time John asked God to forgive him for not believing in His total forgiveness. He praised and thanked God for the peace that came over him. He knew that God had forgiven him, and his spirit was healed when he was at last able to forgive himself.

Others

The story of Leonardo da Vinci, the famous fifteenth century Italian artist, is a good illustration of the need to forgive others. Da Vinci had a violent quarrel with a fellow painter shortly before he began work on *The Last Supper*. As he began to paint, his anger led him to paint the face of the man who was now his enemy into the face of Judas. This was da Vinci's revenge, and he was gleeful over what he had done.

He painted the other disciples and was pleased with his work; but when he started to paint the face of Christ, his best efforts failed. He could no longer see the Savior he longed to honor. Through his struggle, he realized that he must forgive his fellow painter and erase his face from that of Judas. Only then was da Vinci able to see Jesus clearly and paint His face onto the canvas of *The Last Supper* which generations have acclaimed.

Like da Vinci, we too have difficulty seeing Jesus clearly when the sin of unforgiveness comes between us and someone who has offended us. A colleague may have questioned a decision we made in a committee meeting. A friend may have hurt us by breaking a confidence. A spouse may have spoken harshly at a time when we needed comfort. Anger and hurt and bitterness occur most often in close relationships. Parents may have a hard time forgiving their children or children forgiving their parents. Incest, divorce, drugs, and alcohol can easily be catalysts for deep hurts which may take years to heal. Jesus calls us to forgive—again and again and again—those who cause our pain. When asked how often we should forgive, Jesus said, "'I tell you, not seven times, but seventy-seven times'" (Matt. 18:22).

The Book of Hosea is a story of forgiveness. The prophet Hosea married a woman named Gomer who committed adultery many times. The Lord said to Hosea, "'Go, show your love to your wife again, though she is loved by another and is an adulteress'" (Hos. 3:1). Evidently Gomer had by this time become a slave, but Hosea bought her back for fifteen shekels of silver and some barley. While the story of Hosea is a parable of God's unfailing love and forgiveness of His people, it is also a story of the total forgiveness which He expects us to have for those who hurt us.

I had lunch with a beautiful Christian woman today who was hurting because her son was in jail for drunk driving. He had been sentenced to three years in prison. Helen said, "This incident has turned my son to the Lord. He called me and is sorry for the way he has been living and the hurt he has caused me. He's open to learning all he can about Jesus. He's excited about living for Him." Helen's eyes were shining because she had forgiven her son. Her eyes were on the future—not the past.

So it must be with us. Our God's plan for His people moves steadily forward. Refusing to forgive those who have caused us pain in the past can only hinder His plan for our lives and the advancement of His kingdom.

How Should We Forgive?

Asking for Forgiveness

We don't have to worry that we might forget to ask forgiveness when we get angry with a friend for trying to correct us, or when we gossip or criticize, or cheat. There was a time in my early walk with God that I laid awake at night trying to recall everything I did that day which might not have been pleasing to Him. I wanted to be sure that I didn't forget to ask forgiveness for any wrong doing. I no longer do that. If we are in God's family, we have the Holy Spirit to remind us. We just need to be sensitive to His leading and quick to obey.

No matter how much I want to please God, I do things that I know are not right. It is then that I hear the Spirit's prompting: "You shouldn't have said that. Don't you see you've hurt your friend?" Or, "I see the cashier gave you a dime too much. Being in a hurry is no excuse for keeping it." Or, "Yes, you should have spoken up when the man used your Lord's name in that way—but you didn't." At these times I know I must act to correct the problem I've caused. Then I must go to my Father in true repentance and ask His forgiveness.

God's forgiveness is complete. "As far as the east is from the west," King David wrote, "so far has he removed our transgressions from us" (Ps. 103:12). When we come to our Father in sincere repentance asking for forgiveness, He will forgive us.

We know the words of John are true and they are a comfort to us today: "If we confess our sins, he is faithful and just and will forgive us our sins and purify us from all unrighteousness" (1 John 1:9).

Giving Forgiveness

Forgiving others is an important step not only in our healing from hurt but in their continued growth in Jesus Christ. Too often the response when a wrong is committed is, "Oh! I'm sorry!" And it may carry little meaning.

When our daughter Cindy was in high school, she was not allowed to stay out past eleven o'clock at night when she had a date except on special occasions. We noticed that the time was slipping—from 11:00 to 11:15 to 11:30. Always her response was, "I'm sorry!" And she was off to bed happy and contented. Finally her dad and I had a talk with her. We pointed out that we loved her very much and worried when she was late. Even more importantly, she was breaking the rules, disobeying us, and not being honest with herself in her repentance. Her attitude changed, and she agreed to call us if anything prevented her arriving home on time.

A good friend in our church once hurt me deeply when she turned her back on me because of a misunderstanding. Later Clara came to me and said, "I'm sorry for everything. I love you so much, and I miss you." We held each other close and cried together. I knew the misunderstanding was resolved. We'd never mention it again.

Never mention it again. Those are key words. Important words. Forgiveness must be complete. It must come from the heart. We must put all thought of the wrongdoing from us and begin anew. That's what God does for us. That's what we must do for ourselves and for others.

At the 1995 National Prayer Breakfast at Vandenberg Air Force Base I heard Father Jenco, a Catholic priest, chart his journey to forgiveness. He was abducted by Shiite Moslem extremists in West Beirut, Lebanon, in 1985 and spent nineteen months in captivity. "During that time," Father Jenco said, "I wrote down all the Scriptures on forgiveness. Easy to write them down. Hard to make them real in my life." After much prayer and soul searching this gentle man forgave his captors. Then he was able to say to us, "Forgiving is a liberating experience. Only after I was able to forgive those who had caused me such pain, only then could I move into the future. When I could be grateful for the growth, the understanding of the pain, then I knew I was healed."

If we are unable to do this, we may indeed suffer the consequences in our own lives and, like my Uncle

Jonathan, pass along the results of unforgiveness to those who follow us.

Discovering His Plans

1. Give three good reasons why we should forgive others.

2. Why do you think we sometimes have a hard time forgiving ourselves for things we have done wrong?

3. Explain the unforgivable sin (see Mark 3:20–29). How can we know that we have not committed this sin?

4. What is God's plan for reminding us that we need to ask for forgiveness?

5. Think back to a time you had a hard time forgiving someone. How did you feel as you were struggling with the problem? How did you feel after you had forgiven the person?

14

No Compromise

Occasionally I go back and reread C. S. Lewis's book *The Great Divorce* because I need to be reminded of its lesson. In God's plan there is no compromise between God's good and the world's evil. Lewis states it clearly: "It is still either-or. If we insist on keeping Hell (or even earth) we shall not see Heaven; if we accept Heaven we shall not be able to retain even the smallest and most intimate souvenirs of Hell."[1]

We may have tried to walk with one foot in the kingdom of the world and the other foot in the kingdom of God. Eve tried it. She was convinced that she could have her fruit and still live in the presence of God, but God didn't allow compromise. Cain tried it. He offered grain as a sacrifice rather than the blood sacrifice God commanded. Unacceptable. The Israelites tried it. They talked Aaron into forming a golden calf as their god even though God had said, "'You shall have no other gods before me.'" God's anger burned against His people.

Jesus made a sharp division between the kingdom of God and the kingdom of Satan, between light and darkness. It is true that believers live and walk and move in the world that Satan now rules; but, spiritually, Jesus said those who follow Him "are not of the world" (John 17:16). We are here to reflect the light of Jesus in a world of darkness. The world has undergone many changes since God created it, and it is moving toward even more rapid change. As believers, however, we know that those things which affect humankind for all eternity will never change. God has not changed. The same God who walked with Adam and Eve in the garden of Eden still has dominion over heaven and earth. God's Word has not changed. His Word was tested in that garden, and it stood the test. God's plan has not changed. When Adam and Eve disobeyed God and sin entered their lives, God initiated His plan for a sacrifice to redeem His people. God, His Word, His plan—these are the believer's firm foundation. On the truths embodied in them, there can be no compromise for the one who has his feet firmly planted in the kingdom of God, who is a member of God's own family.

However, this does not mean that we will not be tempted to deny God, to listen to false teachers who question the truths of our Bible, to try in every way to change God's plan. If we believe God, then we know Satan exists and is at work in the world. Be encouraged! "God's solid foundation stands firm, sealed with this inscription: 'The Lord knows those who are his.'" We know He will help us as we resist the temptation to compromise. At the same time, we know that "Everyone who confesses the name of the Lord must turn away from wickedness" (2 Tim. 2:19).

Let's consider the problem of compromise as it relates to (1) God Himself, (2) God's Word, and (3) God's plan.

God Himself

Compromise in Babylon

Let me take you back to 608 B.C. for a visit to the court of Nebuchadnezzar, king of Babylon. When Jerusalem fell, four young Jewish men were brought to this strange land and trained for three years as servants to the king. One of them, Daniel, was given a high position in charge of all the wise men of Babylon because he was able to interpret one of the king's dreams. The other three young men, Shadrach, Meshach, and Abednego, also worked in the palace. They were four brave men, faithful to the God of their fathers. Soon their faith would be tested.

King Nebuchadnezzar was a proud man. He ordered workers to make a gold image of himself, ninety feet high. People throughout the kingdom were ordered to fall down and worship the image. Some Babylonian astrologers happened to notice that Shadrach, Meshach, and Abednego did not fall before the image. They did not worship the golden idol. Quickly the astrologers reported the young Jews to Nebuchadnezzar, and the angry king ordered them to be brought before him. "'What god will be able to rescue you from my hand?'" he asked. They were in a tight spot, but note their reply: "'O Nebuchadnezzar, we do not need to defend ourselves before you in this matter. If we are thrown into the blazing furnace, the God we serve is able to save us from it, and he will rescue us from your hands O king. But even if he does not, we want you to know, O king, that we will not serve your gods or worship the image of gold you have set up'" (Dan. 3:16–18).

These three young men did not compromise. They stood strong for God. Although they were thrown into the fiery furnace, God sent an angel to rescue them.

Daniel's turn to be tested came later during the reign of King Darius. The king issued a decree that for thirty days anyone who prayed to any god or man except him would be thrown into the lions' den. Daniel's practice was to pray to God three times daily kneeling by his upstairs window. One day some jealous administrators saw him and reported him to the king. The king liked Daniel and was greatly distressed. Nevertheless, he could not rescind the sentence. Daniel was thrown into the lions' den. Again God was faithful to one who refused to compromise. An angel shut the mouths of the lions, and Daniel walked out of the den the next morning unharmed.

In both instances, God was honored because four men refused to compromise and worship other gods. Both Nebuchadnezzar and Darius praised the one true God, the God of Daniel, Shadrach, Meshach, and Abednego.

Compromise of Our Worship Today

However, God does not always save us from persecution when we stand strong and refuse to compromise. Many Christians in the early church met death when they refused to bow their knees to Caesar. Many Christians today choose death rather than bow to other gods.

For those of us who live in countries where freedom of worship is taken for granted, the temptation to compromise and worship false gods is more subtle. We may even have difficulty identifying our idols, but whoever or whatever takes top priority in our lives can become an idol—a god. God's Word is clear: "'You shall have no other gods before me. You shall not make for yourself an idol in the form of anything in heaven above or on the earth beneath or in the waters below. You shall not bow down to them or worship them; for I, the LORD your God, am a jealous God'" (Exod. 20:3–5).

We must not worship people. In a recent article in *Moody* magazine, Doug LeBlanc pointed out that many Americans teeter on the brink of compromise by their "unusual degree of attention to the world of sports." The gods of sports fall. LeBlanc reminded us that Greg Louganis, Pete

Rose, and Magic Johnson—all once American heroes— have disappointed us. On a wide scale we have seen the greed of players and team owners in the world of sports as they have disputed contract negotiations.[2]

In the same way, those in the world of politics, enter- tainment, academic studies, even those in church leader- ship, will not stand the test of being worshiped as gods.

We cannot hold humans up as glorified heroes lest we find ourselves adding other gods to our worship of the one true God. Only Almighty God is worthy of worship.

We must not worship false sources of knowledge. Sometimes our gods of compromise are found in our sources of knowledge. Tony Schwartz describes the electronic media as "the second god." Kenneth Myers sees some truth in this and writes: "If not omnipresent, the electronic media are anywhere we want them to be. If not omnipotent, they have substantial social and political power. If not omni- scient, they are nonetheless the source of all sorts of knowledge for many people. If not eternal, they do . . . have a certain timelessness."[3]

Do we seek more knowledge from our television set, secular books, newspapers, and magazines than we do from God's Word? Do we place more trust in what we take in from these media than we do in what God makes clear to us in our Bible? If we do, we may be in danger of compromising our worship.

We must not worship money or material things. Greed for money and love of material things can also move us away from our God and cause us to compromise if we're not watchful. Jesus said, "No one can serve two masters. Either he will hate the one and love the other, or he will be devoted to the one and despise the other. You cannot serve both God and Money" (Matt. 6:24). It is "either-or."

In a recent issue of *Newsweek*, Jerry Sheler wrote an article titled, "Is God Lost as Sales Rise?" Sheler quoted Carl Henry, a highly respected eighty-two-year-old theologian, as he wandered through the exhibits at the Christian Booksellers Association Convention. "If the ancient prophets could see some of the crass commercialism conducted in the name of God today," Dr. Henry said, "they would probably weep."[4]

I don't remember having anything with Christian symbols except my Bible and a gold cross on a chain until a few years ago. Now as I look around my office I see a brass plaque with the word *JOY* on it. A wooden cross which my husband made for me hangs on the wall along with an autographed picture of Ken Taylor. A number of Scripture verses, given to me by family members and other special people in my life, are framed and hanging on the wall. Sitting on a shelf is a pair of carved wooden hands held together, praying, given to me by a group of IVCF students. Around my home are many more things that remind me that I am a Christian.

The items which grace our homes with Christian symbols are a great blessing. So are Christian bookstores. But Carl Henry's words serve as a warning to us that we must never allow possessions or money to become idols. We cannot allow them to take the place of God in our lives by placing too much value on them.

Are you as troubled as I am about the many gods that can so easily creep into our lives? We may indeed be tempted toward hero worship. Or we may find that we give more attention to earthly sources of knowledge than we do to God's truth. Or we may place greater value on making money and acquiring material things than we should. God's Spirit has been given to believers to warn us of the danger of other gods in our lives.

We can only worship one God, Creator of heaven and earth, the One who loves us. He will not share His worship or His glory.

God's Word

A Priceless Gift

I often look at my bookshelf and see all the Bibles lined up—the King James Version, New King James Version, New International Version, New American Standard Version, and several others. I'm so thankful for God's Word. It is a priceless gift to us, His family. In it I can find everything I need to know about God and how He wants me to live my life. "All Scripture," Paul wrote, "is God-breathed and is useful for teaching, rebuking, correcting and training in righteousness, so that the man of God may be thoroughly equipped for every good work" (2 Tim. 3:16–17).

When the Spirit led Jesus into the desert to be tempted by Satan, He had not eaten for forty days. He was hungry. When Satan suggested that Jesus turn stones into bread to satisfy His hunger, Jesus replied, "'It is written: "Man does not live on bread alone, but on every word that comes from the mouth of God"'" (Matt. 4:4). Jesus quoted from God's Word—Deuteronomy 8:3, which was familiar to the people in His day. God's Word is our bread, our meat, our life.

The Old Testament's thirty-nine books contain the history of God's people from the beginning, and in poetry and prophecy clearly point to the coming of Jesus the Messiah, our Savior. The four Gospels of the New Testament tell us of Jesus' birth, His ministry, His teaching, His sacrifice, and His victory over sin and death. The remaining twenty-three books tell us about the Church of Jesus Christ through history and letters. God's plan. From Genesis through Revelation, His plan is laid out for us. It's all there in His Word.

While God continues to open His Word to us through His Holy Spirit, the written word is complete. As evangelical Protestant Christians, we believe that the canon was closed with the sixty-six books we now have and nothing more is to be added. Note the closing words in the last book to be written:

I warn everyone who hears the words of the prophecy of this book: If anyone adds anything to them, God will add to him the plagues described in this book. And if anyone takes words away from this book of prophecy, God will take away from him his share in the tree of life and in the holy city, which are described in this book.

He who testifies to these things says, "Yes, I am coming soon."

Amen. Come, Lord Jesus.

The grace of the Lord Jesus be with God's people. Amen. (Rev. 22:18–21)

Not only is God's Word complete, but it has unity. This became clearer to me when I began to see the thread of God's plan woven through the books by the use of repeated themes. Beginning in Genesis, the themes of covenant, obedience, altar, sacrifice, shepherd, and numbers interlace and weave their way to the New Testament where they all come together in the story of the New Covenant. Other themes appear in surprising places to help us remember that they are important ideas in God's plan. For example, the tree of life in the garden of Eden appears again in the last book of the Bible. There in Revelation 2:7 Jesus says, "'To him who overcomes, I will give the right to eat from the tree of life, which is in the paradise of God.'" God was surely watching over His Word. Only by divine inspiration could our Bible, written over a period of 1,600 years through the work of more than forty men, have such completeness and unity.

James I. Packer wrote: "A Bible that can be read and trusted by all Christians as straightforward instruction from God Himself about His relation to His world and everything in it is a precious gift, one that the church and, indeed, the human race needs."[5]

The completeness, the unity, the beauty of God's Word as it reveals God's plan to us brings praise and thanksgiving to our hearts for this priceless gift of His love.

The Temptation to Compromise

If you are as busy as I am, you may sometimes be drawn away from God's Word by work, social life, television, or any number of things which gobble up time. Yet we both know that we are commanded to study God's Word. We must be ready to stand before Him as "a workman who does not need to be ashamed and who correctly handles the word of truth" (2 Tim. 2:15). If we are compromising to the neglect of God's Word, then we need to make some changes in our daily plan.

Jenny Lind did. She made her debut as an operatic singer when she was only eighteen and was a great success. However, at the height of her career she left the stage and never returned to it. When asked why she gave up all the esteem, popularity, and money, she replied, "When every day it made me think less of this (laying a finger on the Bible) and nothing at all of that (pointing to the sunset), what else could I do?"[6]

Even more serious is the temptation to compromise what we know to be true about the inerrancy, the completeness, the unity of God's Word. In my neighborhood are several Mormon families. They believe that God revealed new "truth" to Joseph Smith Jr., and that He continues to reveal new "truth" to certain living prophets in their church. Knowing that I am a writer, one of my neighbors brought me a copy of the King James Version of the Bible which has explanatory notes and cross references to the *Book of Mormon, Doctrine and Covenants*, and *Pearl of Great Price*—three books that the Mormons believe contain new "truth" to add to God's words. I wanted to be my neighbor's friend, but I had to tell her that the books in my Bible are without error. God has not added any new truths to them.

Walter Martin wrote that a cult is "a group of people polarized around someone's interpretation of the Bible and is characterized by major deviations from orthodox Christianity"[7] This is true of the Mormons. It is also true of Jehovah's Witnesses, a group started by Charles Russell, who gave his people a corrupt translation of Scripture and numerous publications expressing his own interpretation. It is true of Christian Science worshipers who see the Bible as corrupt and inferior to Mary Baker Eddy's writings. It is true of many other cults who have continued to rise and fall and draw believers away from God and His Word.

Jesus warned that as the time for His return draws nearer, "'many false prophets will appear and deceive many people'" (Matt. 24:11). I often think of the words God gave to the prophet Hosea. I believe they are meant for us: "'My people are destroyed from lack of knowledge'" (4:6). We must be faithful students of God's Word to avoid being misled and to help those who need to know the truth. We cannot compromise on these important issues related to the truth of God's Word.

God's Plan

The Apostles' Creed is a statement of beliefs that dates back to the second century A.D. You are probably familiar with it. It reads like this:

> I believe in God the Father Almighty, and in Jesus Christ, His only Son, our Lord, who was conceived of the Holy Spirit, born of the Virgin Mary, suffered under Pontius Pilate, was crucified, dead, and buried. The third day He arose again from the dead and sitteth on the right hand of God the Father. From thence He shall come to judge the quick and the dead. I believe in the Holy Spirit, the Holy Catholic Church, the forgiveness of sins, the communion of saints, and the life everlasting.

God fulfilled His plan to save us by sending His only Son, Jesus Christ, to die on the cross in our place. He paid the price for all our sins that we might come into the family of God through His grace. He is the only way to God.

There is no other. The apostle John explained this to us: "God has given us eternal life, and this life is in his Son. He who has the Son has life; he who does not have the Son of God does not have life" (1 John 5:11).

Think of a deep chasm separating us from God. Then picture the cross of Jesus Christ placed across that deep chasm. It is the only bridge between God and man. We cannot cross any other way.

Still, many people try. I was in Phoenix in May of 1995 and picked up a copy of the *Tribune* newspaper. In the religion section I found a story about Rev. Joan Price who had just become the pastor of Sun Lakes' All Faiths Church. I was surprised at some of this pastor's comments and saddened when I thought of all the people she would influence. "I believe in some of the principles of just about every faith I have studied," she said. "I am grateful for the teachings of all of the masters. My own personal favorite 'guru' is Jesus of Nazareth." She went on to say that she would do a series of sermons on the noble eightfold path of Buddha in the coming weeks and that the Easter service which she led was "very Christian."[8]

I was dismayed to read in the Barna report, *What Americans Believe*, that 37 percent of church attenders agreed strongly that "Christians, Jews, Muslims, Buddhists, and others all pray to the same God, even though they use different names for that God."[9]

In our nation today, it is not easy for those of us who stand firmly on the truths of our Bible to profess that we worship the only true God. It can mean ridicule, persecution, and losing friends. But can we sit back and fail to tell unbelievers that God and His plan of salvation cannot be changed or that Jesus is our only Savior? I cannot forget the words of Jesus when He called the crowd and the disciples to Him and said, "'If anyone is ashamed of me and my words in this adulterous and sinful generation, the Son of Man will be ashamed of him when he comes in his Father's glory with the holy angels'" (Mark 8:38).

No, standing up for what we know to be true is not always easy. And it is not easy for our children. At the moment a family in our church is involved in working out an agreement with our school board to allow their son to sing "Jesus Loves Me" in a class program. Their little boy is only six years of age, a kindergartner, and does not understand why his teacher said no to his selection when he was told to choose his favorite song to sing.

If we are to remain true to God, to His Word, and to His plan, we must not compromise. We cannot expect, wrote C. S. Lewis, that "mere development or adjustment or refinement will somehow turn evil into good."[10]

Discovering His Plans

1. List some issues in our culture which often tempt Christians to compromise? What are some issues on which you cannot compromise and remain true to God?

2. God said, "'You shall have no other gods before me'" (Exod. 20:3). Yet there are many false gods and idols in our culture today. Name some of them. Why do you think people today so freely give worship to these false gods?

3. Name three people whom you greatly admire. How can admiration sometimes turn to worship?

4. What possible danger do you see in continual searching for knowledge to prove the truths of God's Word? What danger do you see in pursuing more and more knowledge about false religions and cults?

5. How would you explain God's plan for saving His people to an unbeliever? Do you see any room for compromise in God's plan? Any other way to enter His kingdom? Any other Savior except Jesus Christ?

15

Guaranteed for Life

Ten-year-old Courtney Kinney is home schooled by her mother at Edwards Air Force Base. One day Courtney's assignment in English was to write a letter to God. Here's what she wrote:

Dear God,
I wonder what heaven is like. I can't wait to go to heaven. When I get there I will get to see Mary, Joseph, John the Baptist, and all the other people in the Bible. I wonder what you look like, God. I love you. I want to see you first of all when I get to heaven. I have so many questions to ask you. I wonder where heaven is. I wonder what the angels look like.

Love, Courtney

Like Courtney, we have questions about heaven. At some time in our lives we have all asked Job's question: "'If a man dies, will he live again?'" (Job 14:14). Job answered his own question with absolute assurance. So can we.

"I know that my Redeemer lives,
   and that in the end He will stand
      upon the earth.
And after my skin has been destroyed,
   yet in my flesh I will see God;
I myself will see him with
   my own eyes—I, and not another.
   How my heart yearns within me!" (Job 19:25–27)

No, death is not the end. Those who are in God's family will live forever in His presence—guaranteed. Before Jesus returned to heaven, He said to the disciples, "'In my Father's house are many rooms; if it were not so, I would have told you. I am going there to prepare a place for you. And if I go and prepare a place for you, I will come back and take you to be with me that you also may be where I am'" (John 14:2–3). That's His plan.

Jesus made it clear that we cannot know when He will return. "'No one knows about that day or hour,'" He said, "not even the angels in heaven, nor the Son, but only the Father'" (Matt. 24:36). We are, however, given signs which Jesus said would become evident to us as the end of this age draws near. One day as Jesus was leaving the temple in Jerusalem, He said to His disciples:

"I tell you the truth, not one stone here will be left on another; every one will be thrown down. . . .

"Watch out that no one deceives you. For many will come in my name, claiming, 'I am the Christ,' and will deceive many. You will hear of wars and rumors of wars, but see to it that you are not alarmed. Such things must happen, but the end is still to come. Nation will rise against nation, and kingdom against kingdom. There will be famines and earthquakes in various places. All these are the beginning of birth pains.

"Then you will be handed over to be persecuted and put to death, and you will be hated by all nations because of me. At that time many will turn away from the faith and will betray and hate each other, and many false prophets will appear and deceive many people. Because of the increase of wickedness, the love of most will grow cold, but he who stands firm to the end will be saved. And this gospel of the kingdom will be preached in the whole world as a testimony to all nations, and then the end will come." (Matt. 24:2–14)

We see our world moving rapidly in these areas today. But "so long as we have the assurance that Jesus Christ is in control, no trial is too great, no storm is too overwhelming, no crisis is too much,"[1] writes Billy Graham. We are simply called to keep watch and to be faithful as God's plan moves forward.

We have nothing to fear. God has revealed the plans He has for us after we leave this earth. In his song, "Until Then," written in 1958, Stuart Hamblen saw life as "a trail that's winding always upward" because "this troubled world is not my final home." Let's look at three things we know God has promised us in His plan for our eternal life.

God's Plan: We Will Live with Him Forever

We Will See Jesus

Jesus said, "'Anyone who has seen me has seen the Father. . . . Don't you believe that I am in the Father, and that the Father is in me?'" (John 14:9–10). Jesus came to show us what God is like. Perhaps that is why my first thought of heaven is that I will see my Savior face to face.

How do you picture Jesus? If you were an artist, how would you paint Him? Many artists have tried to capture on canvas a likeness of Jesus, and some of the most famous have their work in art museums around the world.

One of the oldest Christian works, dating back to the fifth century, is a mosaic of the Transfiguration above the altar in Saint Catherine's Monastery at Mount Sinai. Christ Jesus is pictured in all His grandeur, clothed in a white robe trimmed in pure gold. On His feet are gold sandals. His likeness is slightly larger than life size, but to the viewer standing below and looking heavenward, He appears monumental. Elijah is on the left of Jesus, and Moses is on His right. John and James are kneeling before Him, and Peter lies on the ground at His feet.

In Revelation 1, the apostle John gives us a word picture of Jesus. We wonder why John did not tell us of the glorified Christ he saw at the Transfiguration when he wrote his Gospel, but he didn't. In some ways, however, this omission makes John's vision on the Isle of Patmos even more important. This time only John was present. He alone heard the voice and saw the vision. The crucifixion, burial, and resurrection of the Son of God were past. Jesus was lifted up. Like John, when we see Him, we will see the victorious, exalted, and glorified Christ.

John's vision was a cinerama—both sound and sight. He heard the voice behind him, turned, and saw Jesus in all His glory. John uses the words *like* and *as* in an effort to help us see Jesus as he saw Him: awesome, powerful, and ancient. He appeared to John in the robe of our High Priest. The snow and white wool which John used to describe His hair are symbols of purity as well as great age. The glowing bronze of Jesus' feet remind us of His steadfastness, His permanence, and His strength. The voice John heard was "like the sound of many waters."

What will we do when we see Jesus face to face? John fell at His feet. Then Jesus placed His right hand on His beloved disciple and said, "'Do not be afraid.'" How many times had John heard those tender, loving words?

I know that like John I shall fall at His feet in worship and praise. And I shall not be afraid.

We Will See Our Family

When my mother died, I had a dream which I believe the Lord gave me to relieve the pain of losing her. I saw her as a young girl running through a field of golden wheat to meet my dad. His arms were outstretched, and a big smile was on his face. As Mother reached him, he gathered her in his arms and together they twirled around and around in sheer joy. Mother had been blind for more than forty years. Now she could see! She had suffered with arthritis for many years. Now she was the picture of health, youthful and full of energy. How could I continue to be sad when she had so much happiness?

Imagine the joy of once again seeing those you loved who have gone before you to be with Jesus! The first weekend in September 1989, our church in Lompoc celebrated thirty years of ministry. We spent months planning those two days. Since many of our members come to us from Vandenberg Air Force Base, our people are not always permanent. We sent invitations to former members scattered all over the states. We rejoiced as we opened each response saying, "Yes! We're coming!" And they did. From Florida to California our church family arrived by car, bus, and plane. Everyone was housed in homes. We wanted to be together with those we loved so much.

As we gathered to worship God who had so richly blessed us, the warmth of His love, expressed in hugs and tears of joy as we greeted friends we had not seen in a long time, filled all of us to overflowing. Over and over we heard, "This must be what heaven will be like!" So it will be when we gather with Abraham, Isaac, Jacob, and Joseph, with generations of believers, with family and friends we have known and loved. We will join with the angels in heaven singing praises to our God before His throne.

God's Plan:
God Will Create Everything New

The closing chapters of Revelation, the climax of God's plan, give us a foretaste of what is in store for us. The anticipation of what is to come begins in Genesis 3 when God closed the gates to the garden of Eden, and the anticipation of returning weaves its way through the sixty-six books of God's Word to these last chapters. There, through John's eyes, we see God's creation of a new heaven and a new earth—the New Jerusalem. The brilliance of color, the glorious light, the sense of joy and freedom and fulfillment in the presence of Jesus, the Alpha and the Omega, were almost more than John could bear.

The New Jerusalem: His Family

God's plan comes to completion in a new heaven and a new earth. The prophet Isaiah wrote down God's promise: "'For, behold, I create new heavens and a new earth: and the former shall not be remembered, nor come in to mind'" (Isa. 65:17, KJV). Centuries later Peter wrote, "We, according to His promise, look for new heavens and a new earth in which righteousness dwells" (2 Pet. 3:13, NKJV).

I wonder if Isaiah or even Peter could understand the magnitude of God's promise. John saw what they could only imagine. He wrote, "I saw a new heaven and a new earth, for the first heaven and the first earth had passed away, and there was no longer any sea. I saw the Holy City, the new Jerusalem, coming down out of heaven from God, prepared as a bride beautifully dressed for her husband" (Rev. 21:1–2).

John saw more than a dwelling place. He saw a new relationship. The New Jerusalem is first described as a family, a family built on a perfect relationship. This family is the bride of Christ, His Church. The relationship that humanity lost in the garden of Eden is restored.

Throughout the Bible the sea is a symbol of testing and conflict and fear. Remember the Red Sea in Exodus when God held back the waters that His people might pass through safely? Walking between two huge walls of water was a fearful experience. Remember the Sea of Galilee? On its troubled waters the disciples went through a terrible storm, but Jesus said to them, "'Don't be afraid'" (Mark 6:50). Ancient people did not have the compass and did not dare venture too far from land. The sea was seen as a fearful enemy, but the sea will disappear. All evil will be destroyed. And all fear removed.

Neither will there be any more tears or death or crying or pain. God's people will dwell continually in His presence. Throughout history believers have yearned for this perfect relationship. Paul, who knew God so well, wrote that now we are only able to see "but a poor reflection as in a mirror." However, he knew that some day all God's people would see Jesus "face to face" (1 Cor. 13:12). In his vision, John saw the fulfillment of this desire. "Behold, the tabernacle of God is with men, and He will dwell with them, and they shall be His people, and God Himself will be with them and be their God" (Rev. 21:3, NKJV). Nothing can destroy this relationship.

The New Jerusalem: A Holy City

Some people focus on a literal description of the Holy City, Jerusalem, which the angel showed John. We sing of living in mansions and walking on streets of gold. Others believe that John used symbols to describe the character of the city. It is beautiful, perfect, and holy because there the glory of God shines like precious stones.

John did not see a temple in the New Jerusalem. He wrote, "The Lord God Almighty and the Lamb are its temple." He saw no sun or moon because the "glory of God gives it light, and the Lamb is its lamp." In this New Jerusalem there is no darkness (Rev. 21:22–23).

In the garden of Eden a river divided into four and flowed through the garden to make it fruitful. Now John saw "the river of the water of life, as clear as crystal, flowing from the throne of God and of the Lamb down the middle of the great street of the city. On each side of the river stood the tree of life, bearing twelve crops of fruit" (Rev. 22:1–2). The river of the water of life symbolizes the fullness of the Holy Spirit flowing forth from the throne. The river waters the tree of life which bears fruit—a total feeding of abundant blessing of God's people. When we reach this New Jerusalem, we will have access to all that was lost when sin separated man from the tree of life in the garden of Eden.

God's Plan: Everyone Is Invited

I love to sing, and I look forward to heaven where many voices will join together in singing God's praises. John heard a great multitude singing, "'Hallelujah! For our Lord God Almighty reigns. Let us rejoice and be glad and give him glory! For the wedding of the Lamb has come, and his bride has made herself ready'" (Rev. 19:6–7).

An angel said to John, "'Blessed are those who are invited to the wedding supper of the Lamb!'" (Rev. 19:9). Jesus once told a parable which teaches us that everyone will be invited to this wedding and to the supper which follows. The gospel message will be preached to the ends of the earth before the time for this great gathering of God's people comes. But not everyone will accept the invitation to join God's family, to come to the wedding and enjoy the feast. Listen to the story:

> "The kingdom of heaven is like a king who prepared a wedding banquet for his son. He sent his servants to those who had been invited to the banquet to tell them to come, but they refused to come.
>
> "Then he sent some more servants and said, 'Tell those who have been invited that I have prepared my dinner: . . . Come to the wedding banquet.'
>
> "But they paid no attention and went off—one to his field, another to his business. . . . "

"Then he said to his servants, 'The wedding banquet is ready, but those I invited did not deserve to come. Go to the street corners and invite to the banquet anyone you find.' So the servants went out into the streets and gathered all the people they could find, both good and bad, and the wedding hall was filled with guests.

"But when the king came in to see the guests, he noticed a man there who was not wearing wedding clothes. 'Friend,' he asked, 'how did you get in here without wedding clothes?' The man was speechless.

"Then the king told the attendants, 'Tie him hand and foot, and throw him outside, into the darkness, where there will be weeping and gnashing of teeth.'

"For many are invited, but few are chosen." (Matt. 22:1–14)

On another occasion Jesus explained what will happen when He gathers His family in heaven. He said:

"When the Son of Man comes in his glory, and all the angels with him, he will sit on his throne in heavenly glory. All the nations will be gathered before him, and he will separate the people one from another as a shepherd separates the sheep from the goats. He will put the sheep on his right and the goats on his left.

"Then the King will say to those on his right, 'Come, you who are blessed by my Father; take your inheritance, the kingdom prepared for you since the creation of the world. . . .'

"Then he will say to those on his left, 'Depart from me, you who are cursed, into the eternal fire prepared for the devil and his angels. . . .'

"Then they will go away to eternal punishment, but the righteous to eternal life." (Matt. 25:31–34, 41, 46)

Peter wrote that the Lord is patient, "not wanting anyone to perish, but everyone to come to repentance" (2 Pet. 3:9). But He will not take away our free choice.

Not everyone who is invited will be at the wedding supper of the Lamb. Many will refuse the invitation.

The love of Jesus shines through His words as He reveals the eternal purpose of His plan. His warning is absolutely clear: "'The cowardly, the unbelieving, the vile, the murderers, the sexually immoral, those who practice magic arts, the idolaters and all liars'" will not inherit anything that is planned for believers. They will not be in His family. Rather "'their place will be in the fiery lake of burning sulfur. This is the second death'" (Rev. 21:8).

Believers will never know a second death. I love Jesus' words in John 5:24. It has meant so much to me over the years. "'I tell you the truth, whoever hears my word and believes him who sent me has eternal life and will not be condemned; he has crossed over from death to life.'" To come into His kingdom, we must *hear* the word and *believe.* When we make that choice, we cross over from death to life. We will die physically, but we will never again know spiritual death—the second death.

When John first looked up into heaven, he saw "a door standing open" (Rev. 4:1). And he heard Jesus say, "'Here I am! I stand at the door and knock. If anyone hears my voice and opens the door, I will come in and eat with him, and he with me'" (Rev. 3:19–20). In the last chapter of God's plan, the Spirit and the bride call, "'Come!'" And Jesus says, "Let him who hears say, 'Come!' Whoever is thirsty, let him come; and whoever wishes, let him take the free gift of the water of life" (Rev. 22:17).

As I read through God's Word and see His plan unravel before my eyes, I'm reminded once again of His great love for us. From the very beginning, His desire was for our companionship. He has always loved us. Like a loving father, He is quick to forgive us even when we take detours off the path of His perfect plan for our lives.

I'm thankful for the signposts which appear again and again along the pathway of God's plan, in book after book of His Word. C. S. Lewis wrote, "When we are lost in the woods the sight of a signpost is a great matter." They have led many of us into the family of God. Look these signposts up in your Bible: John 3:16; Romans 5:8; Romans 6:23; John 5:24; and John 20:31.

For those of us who have trusted Jesus and joined His family, signposts still have significance. Lewis explains: "When we have found the road and are passing signposts every few miles, we shall not stop and stare. They will encourage us and we shall be grateful to the authority that set them up. But we shall not stop and stare, or not much; not on this road, though their pillars are of silver and their lettering of gold. 'We would be at Jerusalem.'"[2]

Our God will bring us into that New Jerusalem to live with Him forever, according to the plans of His heart.

Discovering His Plans

1. Job asked, "'If a man dies, will he live again?'" Reread Job 9:25–27. How would you answer the question?

2. What evidence do you see that God's plan is being worked out in our world today?

3. What will you say to Jesus when you see Him face to face? How does the assurance that you will some day see Jesus affect how you live today?

4. Explain the New Jerusalem of God's plan as it relates to the family of God and the Holy City.

5. The tree of life first appears in Genesis 2:9 and reappears in Revelation 21:1. What does this tell you about the guarantee of God's plan?

6. God's plan is that everyone be invited to come into His kingdom through Jesus, but we are told that few will accept the invitation. How does this affect the plan God has for your life today?

7. Consider the personal profile on page 195. What do your answers reveal about your strengths and weaknesses?

God's Plan for My Life

This is a personal profile to help you see areas of strengths and weaknesses in your life. On a scale of 1 (low) to 10 (high) rate yourself on the following. Circle the number which best applies to each item.

Assurance that Jesus Christ is my Saviour.	1	2	3	4	5	6	7	8	9	10
Acceptance of Jesus as Lord of my life.	1	2	3	4	5	6	7	8	9	10
Assurance that my Heavenly Father loves me.	1	2	3	4	5	6	7	8	9	10
Believing that I am a reflection of Jesus.	1	2	3	4	5	6	7	8	9	10
Knowing and using my spiritual gifts.	1	2	3	4	5	6	7	8	9	10
Living in the freedom Jesus gives me.	1	2	3	4	5	6	7	8	9	10
Serving in the ministries to which I am called.	1	2	3	4	5	6	7	8	9	10
Understanding of suffering.	1	2	3	4	5	6	7	8	9	10
Assurance I'm forgiven and forgiving.	1	2	3	4	5	6	7	8	9	10
Attachment to things of the world.	1	2	3	4	5	6	7	8	9	10
Assurance of eternal life.	1	2	3	4	5	6	7	8	9	10
Faithfulness in reading God's Word.	1	2	3	4	5	6	7	8	9	10
Faithfulness in time spent in prayer.	1	2	3	4	5	6	7	8	9	10
Faithfulness in worship in God's house.	1	2	3	4	5	6	7	8	9	10
Desire to follow God's plan for my life with continued growth.	1	2	3	4	5	6	7	8	9	10

Notes

Chapter 1

1. *The World Almanac and Book of Facts* (Mahwah, N.J.: Funk & Wagnalls, 1995), 959.

Chapter 2

1. *The People's Bible*, vol. 1 (London: Hazell, Watson & Viney, 1885), 103.

2. Amei Wallach, *Los Angeles Times* (18 December 1982), part VI, 1–2.

Chapter 3

1. *The World Almanac and Book of Facts*, 305.

2. Russell Chandler, *Racing Toward 2001* (Grand Rapids: Zondervan, 1992), 47, 119–20.

3. *The World Almanac and Book of Facts*, 964.

4. Ibid., 216.

5. Lesslie Newbigin, *Honest Religion for Secular Man* (Philadelphia: Westminster Press, 1966), 46.

6. Michael Green and R. Paul Stevens, *New Testament Spirituality* (Guildford Surrey, England: Eagle, 1994), 147.

Chapter 5

1. Chandler, *Racing Toward 2001*, 95.

Chapter 7

1. Oswald Sanders, *The Pursuit of the Holy* (Grand Rapids: Zondervan, 1972), 33.

2. Jon Johnston, *Christian Excellence* (Grand Rapids: Baker, 1985), 164–65.

Chapter 8

1. Walter Wangerin Jr., "The Making of a Minister," *Christianity Today* (17 September 1982), 16–18.

2. Dr. and Mrs. Howard Taylor, *Hudson Taylor's Spiritual Secret* (Chicago: Moody, n.d.), n.p.

Chapter 9

1. David Watson, *Called and Committed* (Wheaton, Ill.: Harold Shaw, 1982), 32.

2. Chuck Colson, *The Body* (Dallas: Word, 1992).

3. George Barna, *What Americans Believe* (Ventura, Calif.: Regal Books, 1991), 175, 204, 223.

4. *Christianity Today*, 6 March 1995, 54.

5. Colson, 124.

6. Chandler, *Racing Toward 2001*, 184.

7. Ibid., 188. Quoting Timothy J. Chandler, "Christian Science and Mormonism: Two Alternative Worldviews in American Religion," manuscript delivered at the California Institute of Technology, Pasadena, 23 March 1991, 2.

Chapter 11

1. Billy Graham, *Storm Warning* (Dallas: Word, 1992), 100.

Chapter 12

1. Scott Harrup, "A Century of Martyrs," *Pentecostal Evangel*, 9 April 1995, 26.

2. Kendrick Strong, *All the Master's Men* (Chappaqua, N.Y.: Christian Herald Books, 1978), 118, 163–64.

3. Billy Graham, *Hope for the Troubled Heart* (New York: Walker and Co., 1991), 53.

4. Paul Brand and Philip Yancey, *In His Image* (Grand Rapids: Zondervan, 1984), 282–83.

5. Amy George with Al Janssen, *Goodbye Is Not Forever* (Eugene, Oreg.: Harvest House Pub., 1994), 308–309.

6. Deitrich Bonhoeffer, *The Cost of Discipleship*, rev. ed. (New York: MacMillan Pub. Co., 1949), 201.

Chapter 14

1. C. S. Lewis, *The Great Divorce* (London: HarperCollins Publishers Limited, 1946), 6.
2. Doug LeBlanc, "Culture Watch," *Moody*, June 1995, 27.
3. Kenneth Myers, *All God's Children and Blue Suede Shoes: Christians and Popular Culture* (Wheaton, Ill.: Crossway Books, 1989), 162.
4. Jerry Sheler, "Is God Lost as Sales Rise?" *Newsweek*, 13 March 1995, 63.
5. James I. Packer, "Thirty Years' War: The Doctrine of Holy Scripture," in *Practical Theology and the Ministry of the Church 1953–1984*, ed. Harvie M. Conn (Phillipsburg, N.J.: Presbyterian and Reformed Pub. Co., 1990), 43.
6. Mrs. Charles E. Cowman, *Springs in the Valley* (Minneapolis: World Wide Pub., 1980), 261.
7. Josh McDowell and Don Stewart, *Handbook of Today's Religions* (San Bernardino, Calif.: Here's Life Pub., 1983), 17, quoting Walter Martin, *The Rise of the Cults*, 12.
8. Kelly Ettenborough, "Pastor Completes Journey of Several Faiths," *Tribune*, 6 May 1995, E3.
9. Barna, *What Americans Believe*, 212.
10. Lewis, 5.

Chapter 15

1. Graham, *Storm Warning*, 30.
2. C. S. Lewis, *Surprised by Joy* (New York: Harcourt, Brace & World, Inc., 1955), 238.

Bibliography

Anderson, Leith. *A Church for the 21st Century.* Minneapolis, Minn.: Bethany House, 1992.

Barna, George. *What Americans Believe.* Ventura, Calif.: Regal, 1991.

Chandler, Russell. *Racing Toward 2001.* Grand Rapids, Mich.: Zondervan, 1992.

Cetron, Marvin and Owen Davies. *American Renaissance.* New York: St. Martin's Press, 1989.

Colson, Charles. *The Body.* Dallas: Word, 1992.

George, David C. *Layman's Bible Book Commentary,* vol. 21. Nashville, Tenn.: Broadman, 1979.

Graham, Billy. *Hope for the Troubled World.* New York: Walker and Co., 1991.

———. *Storm Warning.* Dallas: Word, 1992.

Green, Michael and R. Paul Stevens. *New Testament Spirituality.* Guildford, Surrey: Eagle, 1994.

Guinness, Os. *Dining with the Devil.* Grand Rapids, Mich.: Baker Book House, 1993.

Guthrie, Donald. *New Testament Introduction.* Downers Grove, Ill.: InterVarsity Press, 1974.

Hamada, Louis Bahjat. *Understanding the Arab World.* Nashville, Tenn.: Thomas Nelson, 1990.

Howard, David. *By the Power of the Holy Spirit.* Downers Grove, Ill.: InterVarsity Press, 1975.

Howard, Fred D. *Layman's Bible Book Commentary,* vol. 24. Nashville, Tenn.: Broadman, 1982.

Johnston, Jon. *Christian Excellence.* Grand Rapids: Baker, 1985.

Keeley, Robin, Dr. Robert Banks, et al, eds. *Christianity in Today's World*. Grand Rapids, Mich.: Eerdmans, 1985.

Maddox, Robert L., Jr. *Layman's Bible Book Commentary*, vol. 19. Nashville, Tenn.: Broadman, 1979.

McDowell, Josh and Don Stewart. *Handbook of Today's Religions*. San Bernardino, Calif.: Here's Life Pub., 1983.

Morey, Robert. *The Islamic Invasion*. Eugene, Oreg.: Harvest House Pub., 1992.

Mouw, Richard J. *Called to Holy Worldliness*. Philadelphia: Fortress Press, 1980.

Myers, Kenneth A. *All God's Children and Blue Suede Shoes: Christians and Popular Culture*. Wheaton, Ill.: Crossway Books, 1989.

Ogilvie, Lloyd John. *Freedom in the Spirit*. Eugene, Oreg.: Harvest House, 1984.

Ortlund, Raymond C. *Let the Church Be the Church*. Waco, Tex.: Word, 1983.

Osbeck, Kenneth W. *Amazing Grace*. Grand Rapids, Mich.: Kregel Pub., 1990.

Paschall, H. Franklin and Herschel H. Hobbs, eds. *The Teacher's Bible Commentary*. Nashville, Tenn.: Broadman, 1972.

Pfeiffer, Charles F. and Everette F. Harrison, eds. *The Wycliffe Bible Commentary*. Chicago: Moody Press, 1962.

Sanders, J. Oswald. *The Pursuit of the Holy*. Grand Rapids, Mich.: Zondervan, 1972.

Taylor, Dr. and Mrs. Howard. *Hudson Taylor's Spiritual Secret*. Chicago: Moody, n.d.

Wangerin, Walter Jr. *Ragman and Other Cries of Faith*. San Francisco: Harper & Row, 1984.

Woodbridge, John, gen. ed. *More Than Conquerors*. Chicago: Moody Press, 1992.

World Almanac and Book of Facts. Mahwah, N.J.: Funk and Wagnalls, 1995.

Wuthnow, Robert. *God and Mammon in America*. New York: Macmillan, Inc., 1994.

Zacharias, Ravi. *A Shattered Visage*. Grand Rapids, Mich.: Baker Books, 1990.